napkin decoupage

simple • clever • effective

napkin decoupage

simple • clever • effective

deborah morbin • tracy boomer

David and Charles

A DAVID & CHARLES BOOK
David & Charles is a subsidiary of F+W (UK) Ltd.,
an F+W Publications Inc. company

First published in the UK in 2005
Originally published in 2003 by Metz Press, 1 Cameronians Ave, Welgemoed 7530, South Africa

Copyright © Metz Press 2003

Distributed in North America
by F+W Publications, Inc.
4700 East Galbraith Road
Cincinnati, OH 45236
1-800-289-0963

A catalogue record for this book is available from the British Library.

ISBN 07153 2002 5

The author and publisher have made every effort to ensure that all the instructions in this book are accurate
and safe, and therefore cannot accept liability for any resulting injury, damage or loss to persons or property
however it may arise.

Printed in Singapore by Tien Wah Press
for David & Charles
Brunel House   Newton Abbot   Devon

Visit our website at www.davidandcharles.co.uk

David & Charles books are available from all good bookshops; alternatively you can contact our Orderline
on (0)1626 334555 or write to us at FREEPOST EX2 110, David & Charles Direct, Newton Abbot, TQ12 4ZZ
(no stamp required UK mainland).

Text copyright © Tracy Boomer & Deborah Morbin
Photographs © Metz Press

Publisher and editor	Wilsia Metz
Design and lay-out	Lindie Metz
Cover design	David & Charles
Photography	David Pickett, Alchemy Foto Imaging
Production	Andrew de Kock
Reproduction	Cape Imaging Bureau, Cape Town

Contents

Introduction

When we were coerced into writing this book we weren't absolutely convinced that there was even a market for it. However, our publisher informed us that market research had shown that there was definitely a need for it, and that if we didn't do the book, there were others knocking on her door to take on the job. Her powers of persuasion were just too much for us and before either of us could think about the implications we'd signed a contract that gave us only four months to deliver the goods! With traditional decoupage this would have been virtually impossible to do, unless we ignored our families completely for the full four months and gave up some of life's little luxuries – like sleeping or buying shoes. But serviette decoupage is so quick and easy that we realised we could actually get the book done in time, acknowledge our families occasionally and, as an added bonus, grab the odd bite to eat in between! Luckily we are both exceptionally blessed in having wonderful, caring husbands who support us in everything we do (Christopher, we see you've been editing again!).

So here we are then – welcome to the wonderful world of decoupage with serviettes. Serviettes are easy to work with, the selection available is incredible (and growing all the time) and they go onto virtually any surface. Once you start working with serviettes and see how simple it is you'll probably amass a collection of them to rival that of any kitchen or craft shop, exactly as we did. And you will always have beautiful serviettes on hand to use for any catering occasion you can possibly imagine.

In addition to the better known ways of applying serviettes we discuss some 'new' ways of working with serviettes that we didn't cover in our previous book because we hadn't had time to experiment further before its publication. We also decided on a slightly different approach with this book in that it's entirely project-based. You will be given exact instructions on how to make a particular item from start to finish, including colours, fabrics and items needed for each project. We've found with experience that a lot of people phone us up asking for the exact colours and technique that we used "on that lovely bowl on page 61 in your first book". These are always really difficult questions to answer because we probably made the bowl more than three years ago and since then may have made at least 10 more, all with completely different finishes! Hopefully this format will help you to copy things that you really like and inspire you to try new ideas as well.

Finally, bear in mind that doing decoupage for four months non-stop can play havoc with your body and mind. The first thing to go will probably be your neck (followed gradually by the rest of your back). We suggest that you negotiate a discount with your physiotherapist or chiropractor because you may be spending a lot of time there. We realised that our craft was beginning to affect our minds as well when Deborah suddenly shouted out, "Those butterflies will be perfect on a tea-set!" in the middle of her child's school play. What we are trying to tell you, fellow-decoupeurs, is this – take a break occasionally.

Getting started

In this section we cover all the products and items needed to complete the various projects in the book. As we mentioned in our last two books, you really don't have to buy everything at once. Simply select one project that appeals to you and buy the items needed for that project only. Once you've finished, and you're happy with the result, you can move on to the next one. As you do so you'll probably find that you have quite a lot of stuff left over and you can use some of this for the next project, and so on. Slowly, over a period of time, you'll begin to build up a stock of equipment, serviettes and varnishes that will be more than adequate for any other additional items that you may want to make.

The only way that we've learned what does and what does not work is through continual experimenting and this is something we always encourage our students to do. As we've said before, we discuss the products and techniques that work for us. We have had many phone calls from people asking us why we do things one way while they have been taught to do them differently. Our standard response is that people experiment and then choose the methods that work for them.

We try not to get too technical when covering the various items needed for decoupage. We're well aware that most people tend to gloss over chapters like this – but try to keep awake and read everything because we include important hints and tips as we go along, each of which may well prevent a decoupage nightmare. In some instances we have covered the 'pre-preparation' needed

Source material

Considering that this book is about serviettes, you are not going to get confused by the various source materials. The only thing that could confuse you is which serviette to use because there are so many to choose from. A couple of years ago, the choice was really limited – you could either get hideous or more-hideous serviettes – luckily serviettes are obviously selling well, so we nowadays have a wonderful choice. We have also included handmade paper in this section because we didn't know where else to put it.

SERVIETTES

There has been an international trend to move away from traditional decoupage and into serviette decoupage, consequently the serviettes appearing on the market are a decoupeur's dream. It's always better to work with good-quality serviettes because the colours are more vibrant and the paper is a little thicker, making them easier to apply and less likely to 'disappear' into darker backgrounds. Cheaper serviettes are also more likely to tear easily and, very occasionally, the colours may run.

Two drawbacks we've come up against when working with serviettes is that you often have to buy a whole pack in order to use one or two images that you've had your eye on! The next is that it's very rare that you'll find two types of serviettes that complement each other (either with colour or size of images). Between us we've spent a fortune on serviettes and very few of them match. If you should see a serviette that you think might go well with another that you have at home, don't buy it. We eventually learned that it's better if you go home first, fetch the one you have and hold it up next to your intended purchase. You'll save a great deal of money and frustration this way.

Thankfully, a number of craft shops have cottoned on to the booming business of selling serviettes and are separating the packs and either selling them individually or in smaller packs. Don't be too shy to ask your local craft shop if they would consider doing the same thing: the businesses that we've approached to do just that are doing pretty well out of the deal. It may be a little more difficult to persuade the local 'kitchen-shop' to do the same thing though. It would in any case be a good idea to set up some kind of serviette-swap club with fellow crafters who are also probably wondering what to do with the piles of serviettes they'll never use for their craft.

ABOVE *The best way to keep tabs on what serviettes you have brought (and there will be many) is to get yourself a folder with transparent, plastic sleeves and then slot one or two serviettes into each sleeve. By doing it that way you can flip through the folder to find a suitable image without having to haul out your entire stash of serviettes.*

HANDMADE PAPER

BELOW *There is a wide range of handmade paper to choose from that can be used as a background for and to enhance serviette decoupage. Mulberry paper works wonderfully on glass because it is so thin.*

These papers make very interesting backgrounds for serviette decoupage because of their texture. You can use virtually any handmade paper but bear in mind that the thicker the paper, the more difficult it is to work with. Hand-made mulberry paper is an ideal thin paper to work with (especially on glass) because it moulds well and seems to complement most serviette cut-outs. Whatever handmade paper you choose should not be too 'busy' otherwise it will overpower the serviette cut-out and your work will end up looking like a dog's breakfast. Handmade paper is available at many art, stationery and craft shops.

Base materials

Serviettes can be used to decorate virtually anything. The new mediums available for use with serviettes also allow you to decoupage onto bases that were previously 'unworkable' – such as fabric and porcelain. A trip to a junk shop can turn up many wonders that can be given a face-lift with a lick of paint and cut-outs from serviettes.

NEW WOOD/SUPERWOOD/MDF

This is usually the first thing that springs to mind when you begin decoupaging and consequently there is a large and varied selection of wooden blanks available for exactly this purpose. These decoupage blanks don't need much preparation and are obtainable from most craft shops, some hardware stores and at outlets which specialise in selling blanks.

OLD WOOD

Old wooden items can look really good when given a face-lift. The beauty of these items is that they often have a lot more character than the mass-produced superwood items normally sold for decoupage. The drawback of working with old wood is that a fair amount of preparation is involved before you can actually begin decorating it. These items are available in junk shops, garden sheds and your grandmother's house.

OLD METAL

These items always have a certain amount of charm but will also need extra preparation in order to begin decorating them. They can usually be found in the same places that you find wooden items.

GALVANIZED STEEL

Once only available from street vendors and some florist shops, these items are popping up in many craft and decoupage shops. Once again, extra preparation is required before you can start painting them but they are well worth the effort. Maybe it's the delicate, scalloped edges on most of them that give them an almost 'olde worlde' charm but whatever it is they seem to lend themselves to being decorated with romantic images.

BELOW *When decorating items for young children don't worry about overdoing it. Kids love bright colours and texture. These door tags and light switch covers went down a treat because they're bright. Puff paints were used for the writing and to add height to parts of the images. You can use either an entire serviette or cut-outs, depending on your preference.*

CERAMICS

The ceramics used for decoupage are unglazed, bisque-fired items. They are fairly delicate, particularly before they've been decorated, and should therefore be handled carefully.

A completed item can be wiped clean with a damp cloth but not immersed in water – therefore it is not a good idea to serve hot, steaming food in it. They are better suited for dry ingredients, such as nuts or pot-pourri. These ceramics are usually available from potters or various craft shops.

PORCELAIN

This was previously a 'no-go' area when it came to decoupage because the varnishes and paints wouldn't adhere to the surface for any length of time. However, because of the new mediums available nowadays, this is no longer a problem. There are ceramic paints (and porcelain markers) available that can be used and then baked in the oven in order to heat-seal the item. In addition to these there are mediums available to be used over serviettes that can also be heat-sealed, thereby making the object 'usable'. The only drawback is that you need to choose fairly light-coloured porcelain to work on otherwise the serviette image will 'disappear' into the background.

ENAMEL

Enamel objects can be decorated in either the traditional way, where a certain amount of preparation is required, or else treated in the same way as you would porcelain. Should you go for the traditional method, you will be able to paint the background in any way you choose, but the finished item should

ABOVE Plain white porcelain items can be purchased fairly cheaply either as a set or, as in this case, individually. It took us a couple of hours to transform these odd white pieces into a matching coffee set that could rival many of the expensive sets seen in homeware shops. The added advantage of doing this is that your set will be unique and if any items get broken you can easily 'make' a replacement.

They are fairly delicate once decoupaged (if you throw them at your spouse, they'll chip) and are normally purely decorative. If you want to put fresh flowers into a galvanized steel vase, rather put another container inside to hold the water.

GLASS

Numerous glass items can be used for serviette decoupage. Glass can be decorated on either the inside or the outside, depending on the item itself and its end-use. There are products available that can be heat-sealed in order to make the item usable and washable. Glass that has been decorated using traditional paints and varnishes should not be immersed in water because you will eventually ruin the finish. The decorated area should merely be wiped clean.

not be immersed in water and will only really be suitable for storing dry ingredients. On the other hand, enamel items decorated using porcelain medium and serviettes only, are washable and can be used to store or serve any kind of food. Once again, a light-coloured background is preferable for the image to stand out.

FABRIC

The best fabric to use is natural cotton. A cotton/polyester mix can be used but there is a tendency towards 'watermarks' appearing around the image where the medium has been extended, particularly if the fabric is fairly thin. Bleached calico, cotton and bull denim also work well. Serviettes can be applied to other types of fabric but we can't guarantee that they will adhere for any length of time. Items

should be hand washed in lukewarm water but we've had the odd item land up in the washing machine and it came out looking fine. You can even bleach items (provided the fabric can take it) – it doesn't appear to affect the serviette image in any way as long as you don't leave the item in the bleach for too long. Simple embroidery combines very well with decoupage on fabric.

CANDLES

Avoid decorating thin candles unless you want to set the house on fire. When thin candles burn down, the flame can touch the sides of the candle and if it is covered in paper, it's not a good combination! Thicker candles burn down in the centre so this problem is avoided. A plain candle can be decorated with serviette decoupage in a jiffy and we have made and sold many.

BELOW Neither of us had ever done much in the way of embroidery prior to incorporating it into serviette decoupage. However, after a few practice runs on a piece of fabric we were pleasantly surprised with the results. The two crafts seem to compliment each other and could be used on various items such as bed linen and curtains.

Tools & equipment

BELOW *A good way to make use of left-over serviettes is to make greeting cards. They can be as complicated or as simple as you want them to be. This card was made using a simple paper tole method and four serviette images backed onto white paper. Paper tole cards are very popular and children love having a go at making them. We've found that it's a cheap and effective boredom buster during school holidays too!*

Great people, like great ships, sail peacefully in calm and stormy seas

As mentioned in our previous two books, it really isn't necessary to go out and buy all the equipment mentioned in this section unless your name is Bill Gates or you have access to his credit card – in which case we suggest you buy 10 of everything and all of our books too (we need an overseas holiday!). A few basic items are needed for these projects but if you've done any decoupage in the past, you will probably already have them. For those of you who are doing it for the first time, the items are listed in order of importance and we suggest that you refer to the project that you're going to be following in order to find out what is essential.

SCISSORS

Good-quality embroidery scissors are a must for serviette decoupage. They are even more important than the traditional craft knife. Keep them away from little hands and your husband's toenails and they will last forever.

CUTTING KNIFE

We only use our knives for cutting out 'internal bits' and really intricate pieces (such as stems). The reason for this is because, for some reason, serviettes seem to blunt the blade of a knife quickly and we ended up having to replace the blades frequently. The best type of knife to use is a slim craft one – it looks like a scalpel – with replaceable blades. Cutting knives with snap-off blades are not suitable because they lack flexibility. Always change your blade as soon as it becomes blunt or is damaged otherwise you'll tear the serviette.

CUTTING MAT

This is important if you are going to be cutting with a craft knife. A 'self-healing' mat prolongs the life of your blades. Keep it free of paint, glue and varnish – so it won't look like Tracy's – and it should last a long time.

FOAM APPLICATOR AND ROLLER

High-density foam applicators are perfect for decoupage because they don't leave stroke marks. Try to buy the denser kind because they seem to last longer. The other ones become a little floppy after being used a few times.

A foam roller can be used to paint larger items (such as a toy box) but bear in mind that these rollers do tend to give a slightly textured (dimpled) finish to the paint.

BRUSHES

Paintbrushes are useful for painting large areas and can be used in conjunction with foam rollers to get into corners of boxes and shelves. Invest in good quality brushes that don't shed their bristles.

MEDIUM AND FINE ARTIST'S BRUSHES: These are ideal for painting small details and borders. They can also be used to paint the clay edges in elevated serviette technique and the white paper edges in paper tole.

FLAT, SOFT SYNTHETIC BRUSH: This brush is a must for anyone working with serviettes because it is so soft. The type to look out for has golden bristles and, unfortunately, is a little expensive. If you use it exclusively for applying serviettes (don't paint with it) and clean it properly it will last well.

RUBBER ROLLER

A rubber roller is only necessary if you have backed the serviette with white paper or paint because the cut-out is now thicker. It helps to press out excess glue and air from underneath the image. It's also useful for squashing slugs.

GLUES

There are many glues you can use, but experience has taught us that a particular glue simply works best for a particular purpose.

TRANSPARENT PAPER GLUE: This is only used if the serviette has been backed with paper. It is inexpensive and slow drying, enabling you to reposition the cut-out if necessary. Transparent paper glue is available at most stationery stores and some craft shops.

WHITE WOOD GLUE (COLD GLUE): Use this glue to stick down cork or felt onto the bases of your completed items (where necessary) to give them a professional finish. It is also used in conjunction with the elevated serviette technique and to glue down serviettes that have been painted underneath.

BELOW *We wanted to paint the moneybox a dark colour and, in order to prevent the serviette image from disappearing into the background, something had to be done. Separate the layers of the serviette, apply a coat of Podge to the back of the image to be used and then hang it up to dry. When dry apply a coat of white acrylic paint and again leave to dry. Glue it down using white wood glue and a roller.*

LEFT *The wooden file cover was painted with a base coat of broken white PVA paint and then covered with an entire serviette. Remember to take off the hinges before beginning to decorate as it makes your job easier and the end result is a lot cleaner.*

ABOVE *Fridge magnets are easy to make by applying serviette images directly onto air-hardening clay. Try to choose images that aren't too intricate because they can become difficult to work with. Once the clay is dry, you can paint the edges and glue on a magnet using white wood glue. This is another project that children love to get involved in but beware: your fridge will be covered in magnets in no time at all and there'll be no space for shopping reminders for your spouse!*

WHITE FABRIC GLUE: We use this glue, available from most fabric shops, on canvas shoes to give them extra strength because of the battering they will take.

GOLD SIZE: This is the glue used to apply gold or metal leaf. We prefer to work with a water-based product because the varnishes we use over it are also water based. We used to be able to get a wonderful, thin size that worked like a charm but haven't managed to find it for the last two years. The size that we're working with at the moment is a lot thicker and smells suspiciously like white wood glue. It works well but the thinner variety is far superior.

CLEAR SILICON: Silicon is the 'glue' used for paper tole (three-dimensional) decoupage. It creates height and holds the pieces on top of each other at the same time. It is important to buy the correct clear silicon used specifically for paper tole otherwise you could end up with grease marks on your work.

WHITE AIR-HARDENING MODELLING CLAY: This is used for the elevated serviette technique to create height. It dries hard over a period of days, depending on how much is used. Once opened it should be stored in a plastic bag or airtight container in the fridge. It doesn't taste quite as good as Camembert cheese, so don't eat it.

APPLIQUE PAPER

We sometimes use this when working on fabric. It enables you to use less medium and the serviette can be applied without wrinkles. It feels slightly 'rubbery' when finished but then so do many transfers. The paper is sometimes referred to as 'Magic appliqué' and is usually available from shops that stock embroidery items.

BAKING PAPER

Also called Glad-bake, we use this paper in conjunction with the appliqué paper to protect both the serviette and our irons. Make sure you purchase the correct type – it should not be the waxed variety.

SANDPAPER

Most of the projects in this book that require the use of sandpaper should be sanded with either 400- or 600-grit sandpaper. A coarser grade of sandpaper is needed to prepare old painted or varnished wood.

WOODFILLER/SPACKLE

Use to fill in any imperfections on wood or ceramics before you start decoupaging. It may seem unnecessary but it does make a difference to the finished work. These products are water based and easy to sand when dry.

WHITE KITCHEN WIPES

These are the perforated, washable variety. We prefer to use plain white ones because the coloured ones sometimes run. Use them to protect cut-outs when gluing with paper glue and a roller. They're also handy for removing excess glue and varnish.

METAL/GOLD LEAF

True gold leaf costs a fortune and is extremely difficult to work with because it's so flimsy. Many items that profess to be 'gold-leafed' are actually decorated with metal leaf. There are various metallics to choose from, such as gold, silver, bronze and copper. The advantage of using true gold leaf is that it doesn't tarnish over time if it isn't sealed. However, because decoupage normally involves sealing with varnish, this doesn't really apply.

FELT AND CORK

In order to give your completed work a really professional finish, we suggest gluing felt or cork to the base of the item. It also protects the surface on which the item is displayed against scratches. Glue down with white wood glue, leave to dry and trim away any excess pieces.

MISCELLANEOUS ITEMS

These aren't essential but sometimes make life a little easier:

HIGH-DENSITY SPONGE: Sponges come in handy when painting large backgrounds on fabric. The firmer they are the better they work because they don't soak up much paint. You should be able to get one from a craft shop that stocks fabric paint.

METAL RULER: It's preferable to use a metal ruler when cutting straight lines with a craft knife. It not only gives a neat finish: it's impossible to cut a chunk out of a metal ruler like you could from a plastic or wooden one.

WATER-SOLUBLE FABRIC MARKER: Most fabric shops stock these. They are used to mark the position for serviette motifs on fabric.

HB PENCIL: This does the same thing as the fabric marker, except it's used on wood, ceramics and metal.

FUN LINERS: Paint 'pens' can be used on textiles, paper and wood for wording or decoration. They can be heat-sealed and the 'magic' ones give a raised finish adding extra interest to your work.

PRESTIK/BLUE TAC: Two pieces of tac, placed underneath and on top of a serviette, work wonders to separate the layers of serviettes. Simply pull the tac in opposite directions and the layers will come apart immediately.

BELOW *Don't be nervous to work with gold or metal leaf as it's really not difficult and the colours are so rich and vibrant that it's almost impossible to get the same effect with paint. The elephant was perfect to use on a rich gold background but we felt it had to look slightly aged, so we tried not to apply the leaf too evenly and left the imperfections as they were.*

Paint, medium & varnish

There are so many of these available that it's normally a good idea to experiment and find out what works best for you. We don't tend to stick with one brand for everything because we've found that most companies have their speciality, which is precisely why we encourage our students to try out the various options available. As we've said before, don't rush out and buy everything at once. Choose your project and buy accordingly. All the projects described in this book use water-based products that are easy to work with and dry quickly.

BELOW There are few items that are transformed as radically as an old battered watering can. After painting the can, a white wash was applied over the paint to give it a more delicate look. Always take care to avoid runs when painting and varnishing watering cans – they can occur quite easily because of the angles.

PAINT

The first thing to be sure of when buying paint is that it is acrylic or water-based. The easiest way to check whether you are buying the correct type of paint is to read on the container whether brushes can be cleaned with water or if the 'solvent' is water. Should you still be unsure, ask the sales staff.

There are hundreds of different colours of acrylic craft paint to choose from. These come in a variety of small quantities, which are perfect for small projects. Should you be working on a bigger item, though, it is a lot more cost-effective to buy a one-litre tin. We always have a tin of broken white PVA in stock because it is used for base coats and is also a perfect base colour to use for most paint techniques.

We recommend that you try various brands because even though some products are cheaper, you may have to apply many more coats of paint to get a good, even colour. This could end up costing you more in the long run and besides that, it's not that much fun having to apply six coats of paint! There are so many brands to choose from that we've stayed away from using named colours – one company's Heavenly Blue is another's Dirty Grey so unless it's a standard colour we've used our own descriptions.

WATERCOLOUR SET

These aren't used too often, so only invest in a set (or pinch your child's one) if you intend tackling one of the three-dimensional decoupage projects. The paint is used to touch up the white edges of the paper in paper tole and can come in very handy to touch up mishaps when using the elevated serviette technique.

CRACKLE MEDIUM

Don't confuse this with Antique Crackle. In this instance the cracked look is achieved between two layers of paint rather than over a painted surface – it looks almost as if the top layer of paint has split and cracked (which might be precisely what happens but we're not chemists, so we don't know). Any decoration done over crackle should be subtle otherwise the whole thing can end up looking too busy. Try to buy one of the crackles that can be sealed with water-based products because these are easier to work with. This information is usually included in the directions for use on the label.

SCUMBLE GLAZE

Acrylic scumble glaze is a must for most paint finishes because it keeps the paint 'workable' for a longer period of time. It is used in conjunction with paint and water to make up a glaze or wash and the more scumble glaze you add, the longer the glaze will take to dry. This is a bonus when working on a large item which could end up looking blotchy if the paint dries before you have a chance to neaten it up.

Be sure to buy an acrylic scumble glaze to use in conjunction with water-based paints.

FABRIC PAINT

These paints come in a variety of colours and quantities, so buy accordingly. You'll sometimes have to apply two coats of fabric paint (which can

be mixed with fabric paint extender before use) so bear this in mind when purchasing your paint.

There are different types of fabric paint available BUT the best kind to use in conjunction with serviettes is transparent paint. There are two reason for this: the first is that it's cheaper and secondly (but more importantly) serviettes adhere better to this paint. Opaque paint has 'hiding power', which is perfect for painting over dark backgrounds but, without getting too technical, it has more of a 'plastic' feel to it and this interferes with the long-term adherence of the serviettes.

Metallic paints are best used for borders or small details.

ABOVE *This tablecloth was our first attempt at tackling a large painted area on fabric. It's best to work on a table when painting fabric but if you don't have one big enough (like us) the floor works just as well. If you can't face the prospect of painting such a large area buy cream cotton fabric, leave the centre unpainted and just paint on a border before beginning to decorate.*

PODGE

Almost everyone who has ever done decoupage will know what Podge is. It is a water-based varnish that goes on milky but dries clear. We don't use it nearly as much for serviette techniques as we do for traditional decoupage but you will notice it creeping in occasionally. In this book we use Podge mainly to seal paint before applying serviettes. Some people like to use it to apply serviettes but we prefer to use something a little thinner because it makes application easier. If you want to go the traditional route and bury your work in 30 or 40 layers of varnish, we suggest that you do apply the serviette with Podge and continue using it to build up the layers.

A golden rule to remember with Podge is that any other product can go over it but don't try to put it over anything other than water-based paint (or another layer of Podge).

WATER-BASED VARNISH

Water-based or polyurethane varnish is perfect to use as a 'glue' for applying serviettes to most painted items – EXCEPT fabric! It is thin and easy to apply so it doesn't damage the delicate serviette. Like most water-based mediums or varnishes it goes on milky but dries clear. Stir the varnish well before use (especially the matt one) but don't shake it otherwise you'll end up with hundreds of tiny bubbles. If you use this varnish to apply serviettes, continue using it to finish off your project. It's not normally a good idea to switch products once you start working with varnishes because they have this nasty habit of presenting you with some very strange reactions to each other.

FABRIC PAINT EXTENDER

An extender is a cost-effective way of making fabric paint go further. Most fabric paint that you buy off the shelf already has extender in it but it doesn't hurt to add more. Bear in mind that the more extender you use, the more it dilutes the pigment and the lighter the paint will become. The lustre of metallic paint can be affected by the addition of extender so it is worthwhile experimenting with these paints before using them on a project. Once paint and extender have been mixed together, they can be stored as any normal paint in an airtight container. However a metallic paint/extender mix should be used immediately.

LACQUER MEDIUM

Be careful not to confuse this lacquer with the aerosol paint that makes you high within 5 minutes! It is also not the stuff that you spray on your hair. This is a water-based product so the fumes are not nearly so potent. It comes in matt, silk matt and gloss and should also be stirred well before use. It is milky in appearance, dries clear and is weather and light resistant. It can be used on wood, metal, tin, ceramics, cardboard, candles, soap and plastic.

CANDLE MEDIUM

This medium is used on both candles and soap. If the candle feels a little sticky once dry, simply apply a coat of water-based polyurethane or lacquer varnish over it and this will sort out the problem. Candle medium can also be mixed with paint if you wish to paint the candle before decorating it.

PORCELAIN MEDIUM

This is what you need to buy if you want to decorate porcelain and glass and actually be able to wash the finished item. Porcelain medium is used to apply the serviette to the object. Once it's dried it can then be heat-sealed in the oven. The bottles come in various sizes but a little goes a long way. It's best not to wash porcelain or glass decorated in this way in a dishwasher.

TEXTILE MEDIUM

This works in pretty much the same way as porcelain medium in that it can be heat-sealed so that you can wash the fabric when you need to. Textile medium works best on cotton or cotton-mix fabrics. We have found that the thicker and more textured the fab-

ric (like canvas) the better the product works. There is sometimes a tendency on thin, cotton-mix fabrics for some textile mediums to leave a 'water-mark' around the edges of the image. Items should be hand-washed only.

FABRIC-PAINT SEALER

You can use this to seal your finished work (and also to apply serviettes to fabric if you've run out of textile medium). The advantages of using this product are that it gets rid of any stickiness caused by some textile mediums and it seals the paint, thereby giving it a certain measure of protection from dirty marks. The disadvantage is that it does make the fabric (and particularly the serviette images) less flexible. The fabric doesn't quite feel like cardboard but it's markedly stiffer than normal.

ABOVE *Candles covered in serviettes are probably one of the quickest forms of serviette decoupage. These particular candles were textured and the serviette moulded perfectly into the indentations. We prefer to tear the sides of the serviette where the two edges overlap because torn edges blend better and are less noticeable than ones that have been cut.*

LEFT *The border of this serviette was cut down and placed around the edges of the pencil case (in other words, the border became a border again) and a single image, placed off-centre, finished the project. Some items take all day to complete but this took all of 15 minutes.*

21

Preparation

Those of you who bought our last two books (and read them properly!) will already know that we believe a good end result starts with proper-preparation. The beauty of working with serviettes is that the actual decoration of the item takes virtually no time at all – so you have all that extra time on your hands to prepare the items correctly! We have seen, time and again, finished work that falls short because not enough care has been taken with preparation. There are many creative people out there – more so than us – who have wonderful ideas and if they had spent just a little more time on painting and cutting, their work would be stunning. We are occasionally asked by our students how they can achieve the same standard of work as ours. It really is quite simple: be fussy, don't skimp on the preparation and don't take any advice on short cuts from interfering spouses!

This section covers the preparation required for various base materials, as well as cutting techniques. After much contemplation we decided that, even though this book is project-based, it would be better to separate the preparation of various items from the actual projects for two reasons. Firstly, we've noticed that project books that have too much 'text-per-project' can be a little off-putting and confusing and if we included preparation and steps together we feel it could result in this problem. Secondly, by doing it this way the preparation is separated from the rest of the project so you will be able to apply it to various other projects of your own.

Preparing base materials

This is not terribly exciting but it needs to be done to ensure a professional finish (a good idea is to get somebody else to do it). Fortunately, serviette decoupage is in many cases, a lot more 'lenient' than traditional decoupage. In some instances, the preparation required is merely to wipe the base item with spirits or wash and dry it before beginning to work on it. Wood, galvanized steel and enamel (if it is to be painted) need a little more work. It is important to bear in mind that correct preparation is not only required to achieve a good finish but also plays a role in ensuring adhesion of the serviettes and, in the case of wood, a smooth surface that can easily be wiped and does not collect dirt.

NEW WOOD

When we use the term 'new wood' we mean any wood that doesn't have any dirt, grime, varnish or polish on it. The type most commonly used in this country for decoupage is superwood or Medium-Density Fibreboard (MDF). However, pine or virtually any other kind of raw wood should be prepared in this way:

- Apply a base coat of broken-white PVA to the entire surface of the item, inside and out.

- When dry, fill all blemishes and holes with wood filler. Apply the filler as smoothly as possible in order to make sanding easier. Leave to dry.
- Dry-sand the entire item with 400-grit sandpaper, ensuring that there are no rough edges and that the wood filler is smooth. The reason why we sand wooden items after applying a base coat (rather than before) is because water-based products lift the fibres of wood so it's pointless sanding like mad before applying your first coat of paint – you'll only have to do it all over again.

ABOVE *We knew that we had a serviette with herb images at home, so when we came across these wooden herb names, we snapped them up. It's best to paint the lettering before gluing it down because it's easier to get into the corners and you won't get paint on the background. The signs should be sealed with at least 4 coats of varnish if they are going to be used outside.*

OPPOSITE PAGE *This chair was found in a really bad state in a store room, but the time spent preparing, painting and distressing it before applying the serviette cut-outs was well worth the effort. The project is discussed in detail on page 50.*

BELOW *We loved this serviette but knew that it would have to be put on in its entirety because it would have been impossible to cut out. The bin was the perfect size and we painted it the same colour as the background of the serviette so that the edges of the serviette would blend into it. We tore, rather than cut, around the edges to make them blend better. Gold paint was sponged around the scalloped edges of the bin to finish it off.*

If you want to decoupage onto bare wood – without painting the background – replace the base coat with a coat of Podge and leave out the wood filler (unless it blends with the wood). When dry, sand as described above and apply another thin coat of Podge before beginning to decorate.

OLD WOOD

Items with varnished, lacquered, polished or painted surfaces need to be cleaned up properly before you can begin decorating them.

- The object should be wiped down with spirits to remove any wax or grease.
- When dry, sand it down thoroughly with coarse sandpaper, removing anything that shines, sticks or flakes in the process.
- Once this has been completed, sand again with finer-grade sandpaper before you begin decorating it.

- It's a good idea to use a universal undercoat as your base coat because, if there are any areas that still have a little varnish on them, the undercoat will adhere to these sections.

Be sure to check any old wooden items very carefully for signs of borer beetle or wood worm – there's nothing worse than having to spend thousands fumigating your entire house because you've brought these pests into it.

GALVANIZED STEEL

It is imperative that galvanized steel is prepared properly to ensure that the item lasts well. Speaking from experience (we admit it, we didn't follow our own advice!), any short cuts in preparation will eventually become apparent. Therefore, the following steps are necessary:

- Clean the item with galvanized steel cleaner to remove the protective coating and any dirt or grime. Use a stiff metal brush or scouring pad and follow the manufacturer's instructions on the tin.
- Apply a liberal coat of galvanized steel metal-primer but make sure that you don't have any runs. Leave to dry.
- If you managed to get hold of (and have used) one of the primers that doesn't require an undercoat before painting, your preparation is now complete. If not, you will have to apply an undercoat before painting the item with the acrylic colour of your choice. Should you be unsure of the type of primer you have used, read the instructions on the tin – they'll normally advise you as to whether or not an undercoat is needed.

ENAMEL

There is very little preparation involved if you are going to apply serviettes directly onto enamel (without painting it). All you need to do is clean the item with spirits and a soft cloth in order to give you a squeaky-clean surface to work on. However, if you want to paint the enamel before decorating, prepare the surface as follows:

- Dry-sand the item – inside and out – with 100-grit sandpaper in order to 'key' the surface to ensure paint adhesion.

- Apply one generous coat of general-purpose steel-primer to the entire item and leave to dry for 24 hours or according to the manufacturer's instructions.
- Apply one coat of universal undercoat and leave to dry for 24 hours (or less, if the tin says so).

OLD METAL

Whereas old metal is not always covered in paint, it does usually have rust on it somewhere.

- All traces of rust will have to be removed by rubbing these sections down with fine steel wool.
- As with old wood, anything sticky or greasy should be wiped away with spirits.
- Once the item is free of grease and rust, sand the entire object lightly with 600-grit sandpaper.
- Apply a generous coat of metal primer followed by a universal undercoat when dry. Now you can begin decorating as usual.

GLASS AND PORCELAIN

Before beginning to work on either of these base materials, the only preparation needed is to clean them first. You could either wash the item in hot, soapy water or, better still, wipe it clean with spirits and a soft cloth. That's it – it's now ready to be decorated.

BELOW This toddler's potty (which could actually be used in a bathroom to store soap or creams) worked perfectly with the sea shell images because they were virtually the same colour as the rim. Enamel is decorated in the same way as porcelain but bear in mind that it heats up a lot quicker because it's metal, so it doesn't have to be baked as long.

CERAMICS

Sometimes you will come across ceramics – remember we use bisque-fired ones – which need no preparation at all because they are smooth and unblemished. If, however, the item has chips or obvious flaws, these should be filled with spackle or filler, left to dry and the entire item sanded before you can begin painting. A base coat can be applied but it is not normally necessary.

FABRIC

It is best to wash all fabric before beginning to apply serviettes or paint. The reason for this is that many fabrics have a protective 'sizing' on them which helps to keep them clean and this coating can interfere with the adherence of the textile medium or fabric paint. Once dry, the fabric should be ironed before being decorated.

FABRIC PAINTING

All you Fabric Painting Experts out there can skip this section because we only use very basic techniques in this book (and all of you seem to have your own methods and you all believe yours is the correct one!). Before you go though, a tip to remember is that in our experience, opaque paint does not work as well with serviettes as transparent paint because textile medium does not always adhere well to it. As mentioned above, the fabric should always be washed and dried first and the steps for painting are quite simple:

Mix fabric paint and extender together (if you want to add extender). There is no magical or exact formula here – the only thing to remember is that the more extender you use, the lighter the

paint becomes. Always make sure that you have enough paint mixed because it's virtually impossible to mix the same shade again.

If you're painting a large area, it's a good idea to use a high-density sponge to apply the paint. While you're working, stop and blend the painted areas together with a second sponge to prevent your work from looking too 'blotchy'. Smaller areas can be painted with a sponge applicator.

Once the fabric has dried you can decide whether or not it needs a second coat of paint. If it does, then repeat the above step, leave to dry and heat-seal before you begin decorating it. Do this by ironing it on the reverse side with a dry iron (no steam) on a cotton setting. You can also iron over the right side but put a thin piece cloth of over it before you begin ironing.

ABOVE We needed three images the same size for these cups but the serviette we were using only had two so we created an extra one through cutting. The lighthouse was originally twice the size of the other images so we simply cut it in half and replicated the border that was surrounding the boat and the seagull – we do have our moments of ingenuity!

Once we had finished this project, the dog jumped up and left muddy footprints on the apron which would not come out with normal washing – so we soaked it in a weak bleach solution. The muddy footprints disappeared but the images remained in perfect condition. We couldn't believe it either!

An important rule to remember when painting fabric is that you must always have a wet edge.

Painting half an item and then going off to town to meet some friends for coffee, with the intention of finishing it later, is a really bad idea. You will notice where painting has stopped and started again.

Don't be scared to experiment with fabric paint. If you'd like a 'washed' look, a good way of achieving this is to apply the paint to damp fabric and then leave it to dry. Bear in mind that when painting onto damp fabric you won't be able to apply more than one colour to your fabric because the paints bleed into each other.

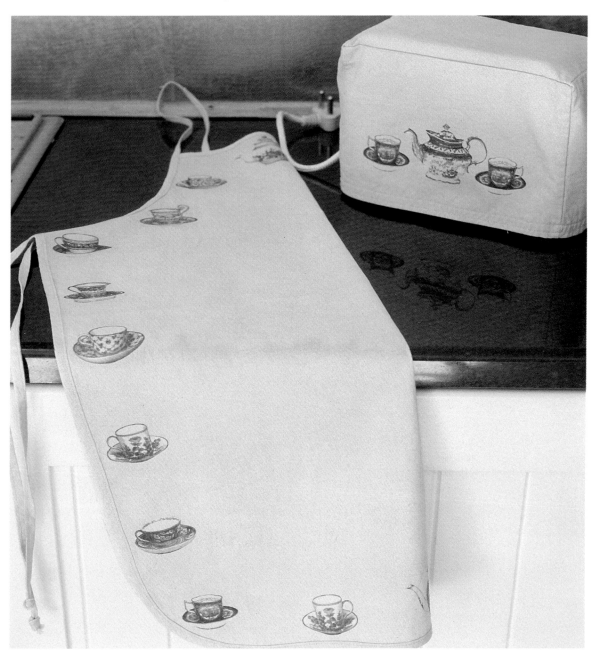

Cutting techniques

The method used to cut serviettes is slightly different from that for cutting paper. For starters, the best advice we can give you is to buy a good pair of embroidery scissors and use these for as much of the cutting as possible. The reason for this is that serviettes have this nasty habit of blunting the blades of craft knives. This is bad news for decoupeurs who normally cut everything with a craft knife but you'll soon get used to working with scissors – as we had to.

Remember that serviettes are delicate and, whether you're using a knife or a pair of scissors, you'll need to work with a gentle hand because it's very easy to tear the paper.

In order to cut serviettes with the least amount of fuss, we recommend following these steps:

• Remove the back layer of the serviette. Most serviettes have three layers and it is only necessary to work with two. The last layer usually comes away easily. If it doesn't, it means you're probably working with a two-layer serviette. If this is the case, leave it. By working with two layers only you save on blades (because sometimes a knife is necessary) and you don't have too many bits of paper flapping around. Don't be tempted to remove both back layers: working with only the top layer is difficult because the paper is so delicate.

• Cut away the inside bits of the image first (this is where it would be easier to use a craft knife). Continue using your knife for any intricate cutting

ABOVE As mentioned before, serviettes are perfect for decorating cards. For this particular one, the serviette image was backed with white paper first to prevent it from disappearing into the dark background. String was used to replace the rope on the original picture and again to add interest.

that cannot be done with scissors. When cutting with a knife press firmly into the serviette rather than pulling the blade along it. As soon as possible, ditch the knife and cut out the rest of the image with a pair of scissors (unless you have an endless supply of blades).

- Finally, separate the last two layers as only the top one is used.

- If they won't separate easily, either slip a craft knife between them or put a little piece of prestik (blue tac) on the top and bottom layer and simply pull – they come apart fairly easily.

You will notice that in some instances we tear around the serviette images instead of cutting. This is only done when the serviette image is too intricate to cut out and the background of the serviette matches the background of the item on which you're working.

The best way to tear around an image successfully is to use the 'wet-and-tear- method':

- Dampen the area around the image by dabbing it with water with a fine paint brush, making sure that the water has penetrated the serviette.

- Now pull gently on these areas – it's a much easier way of controlling the tear. The reason for tearing instead of cutting is that torn edges seem to blend better than cut ones.

Applying serviettes

We've noticed that some of the instructions we've come across on the application of serviettes suggest applying medium to the centre of the image, working upwards and outwards.

This is all very well but, unfortunately, it often leads to uneven stretching and wrinkling, particularly on larger images. What tends to happen is that you end up with a picture that's smooth in the middle and then gets progressively more wrinkled and lopsided at the edges – which is precisely why we don't use this method.

When applying serviettes (once again, particularly large images) a certain amount of wrinkling does take place but, by working from one side of the image to the other, these wrinkles are even – thereby becoming a feature – rather than looking like something that went horribly wrong!

This technique applies to serviette decoupage onto all surfaces. The only one that's slightly different is fabric – the technique is the same but the application of the medium is different. When applying serviettes to fabric the medium must be put on first and then again when you're applying the image. An important rule to remember when heat-sealing serviettes on fabric is to keep the iron moving – if you don't you run the risk of scorching the serviette.

Ensure that you are only working with the top layer of the image. Place it in position (holding it lightly if necessary) and begin brushing medium over it, working from one side to the other. Ensure that your brush is always fairly wet in order to avoid tearing the serviette.

TIPS TO REMEMBER WHEN APPLYING SERVIETTES

- Always extend the medium slightly beyond the image.
- When working on wood, ceramics or painted metal, brush the medium outwards to avoid 'lumps' of varnish drying around the image.
- Wipe away excess medium from around the edges of images that have been applied to porcelain, glass or unpainted enamel. A cloth dampened with spirits will do the trick.
- Serviettes stretch when applied so make allowance for this. If you want to centre an image, first apply medium down the middle of the image then work over to one side and then the other.
- You can use your fingers to push down wrinkles when applying serviettes to fabric but do it carefully and make sure you only work on wet sections, otherwise the serviette will tear.
- When heat-sealing serviette images on fabric, keep the iron moving to avoid getting scorch marks on and around the image.

Specific projects

When we were planning the projects for this book we decided to select as many different bases and techniques as possible in order to give an idea of how serviettes work on various surfaces. Also included are projects that deal with one of the restrictions imposed by working with serviettes – applying them over dark backgrounds.

We've experimented extensively with serviette decoupage and know exactly what can go wrong. Hopefully you won't experience the same problems because we've included tips on how to avoid them.

There are some recently developed methods of applying serviettes that we experimented with but decided not to include in our projects because the problems that they pose outweigh the benefits. One of these methods is to seal the painted or unpainted wood with varnish, leave it to dry and then iron the serviette images into position. The idea is good because the image goes on wrinkle-free. However, as soon as you apply varnish over the image to seal it, it invariably wrinkles! There is also a chance that you could scorch the varnish or the paint when ironing the image onto it. This method does work well on glass, though, because porcelain medium works with the heat and the image doesn't lift when a second coat is applied over it.

Lastly, before you rush head-on into a project we suggest that you read the introduction and handy hints of your chosen project first. Most of the projects require no previous experience with serviette decoupage but some are a little more advanced and it would be better to get a feel for working with serviettes before you tackle these ones.

Topiary bowl

Of all the items we've made in the past, the most popular seem to be bowls, particularly the large enamel ones. The preparation takes a little more time but they are well worth the effort. We decided to give this bowl a fresh, feminine look by using topiary images which work beautifully on a crisp white background. Owing to the fact that the background of the serviette was also white, the images didn't have to be intricately cut out because the two backgrounds blend into each other. This was a real bonus because the images would have been impossible to cut! This bowl was one of our first projects for this book and Tracy's 'bridge ladies' are in the middle of serious negotiations regarding future ownership.

If you are looking to make a gift for someone who likes feminine things, this is definitely it!

1 Prepare the bowl according to the instructions on page 26 for enamel.

2 Use the sponge applicator to apply 4 coats of white craft paint to the entire bowl, allowing sufficient drying time between coats. When dry apply one coat of Podge to protect the painted surface.

3 Arrange the serviette motifs on the bowl. The best way to do this is to apply a tiny piece of prestik to the back of the (non-separated) image and gently press it into position. The prestik also helps to separate the back layer of paper once you remove the motif in order to glue it down.

4 Once you are happy with the arrangement begin gluing the motifs – one at a time – by brushing medium over the dry serviette images with a soft synthetic brush, working from one side to the other. Extend the medium slightly beyond the motif so that it doesn't lift when dry. Leave to dry for 30-40 minutes.

5 Using a soft cloth and a little lavender paint, wipe around the rim of the bowl to create a 'washed' effect.

6 Apply 4-6 coats of medium or varnish to the entire bowl to complete, allowing enough drying time between coats.

YOU WILL NEED
Enamel bowl
White craft or water-based PVA paint
Sponge applicator
Podge
2 topiary tree serviettes – cut (not separated)
Flat soft synthetic brush
Water-based polyurethane varnish or
Lacquer medium for serviettes
Lavender craft paint
Soft cloth
Prestik/blue tac

Cushions

The same serviette was used on the cushions, which were painted white before being decorated. In this instance, we tore around the images instead of cutting them. The border of the serviette was cut out and used to create a border on the cushions. It's best to apply patterned borders in sections because the serviette stretches so much and can be difficult to control.

HANDY HINTS

- In order to balance the design, the same motifs were placed diagonally opposite each other.
- Don't use prestik if you have removed the last layer of paper from the motif. It could tear the serviette and/or leave an oily mark on it.
- Don't take any short cuts with the preparation otherwise the paint may eventually peel off.

- The completed bowl can be wiped clean but don't immerse it in water.
- You can tear around the motifs instead of cutting them – see page 30 for instructions on how to do this the easy way.
- You might as well make several bowls while you're at it – they're so popular that all your friends will want one.

Herbs & flowers bag

1 Using a ruler, measure 40 mm in from the edge of the bag on all four sides and mark the position with the soluble fabric marker. Using these markings as a guide, apply the masking tape to the bag to create the border. Press the tape firmly into position.

2 Place a sheet of plastic inside the bag to prevent the paint from seeping through when you begin painting. Mix lavender paint with equal parts extender and, using a sponge applicator, paint in the border. Leave to dry.

3 Turn the bag over and paint the entire back in the same manner. When completely dry, remove the masking tape, turn the bag inside out and heat-seal the paint onto the fabric by ironing on the reverse side. Use a dry cotton setting for your iron.

4 Cut out a piece of appliqué the same size as the serviette image – don't peel off the backing paper.

5 Place the appliqué onto an ironing board (coarse side facing up) and put the serviette over it, printed side up. Cover with a piece of baking paper to protect the image (and your iron!) and iron the serviette onto the appliqué. Use a dry cotton setting for your iron.

The herb serviette that we used here was one of the smaller sizes that are sometimes available and the dimensions were perfect for the bag. We wanted a lavender background but didn't want to risk losing the 'crispness' of the images which is why we decided to put the images onto the natural background and paint in a border, thereby solving this problem. Don't be put off by having to paint fabric if you've never done it before – it's a lot easier than you might think and often adds life to your work.

6 Trim the edges of the picture using a craft knife and metal ruler. Work out where the images are to be placed onto the bag and make small marks with the water-soluble pen. Peel off the backing paper from one of the images and position it. Cover it with baking paper and iron over it for about a minute in order to 'glue' it to the fabric. Repeat until all the images are ironed on.

7 Apply 2 coats of serviette textile medium to the images, allowing drying time between coats. Extend the medium slightly further than the picture to ensure that the edges don't lift. Once dry, cover the images with baking paper and iron over them to heat-seal.

YOU WILL NEED

1 calico bag
Metal ruler
Water-soluble fabric marker
Masking tape
Plastic sheet
Lavender fabric paint
Fabric paint extender
Sponge applicator
Herbs & flowers serviette – cut and separated
Iron-on magic appliqué
Baking paper
Craft knife
Scissors
Flat, soft synthetic brush
Textile medium

HANDY HINTS

- Use fairly broad masking tape to avoid painting into the area you want to leave plain.
- Ensure that the masking tape is pressed down firmly to the fabric to avoid paint 'bleeding' underneath it.
- Baking paper can be used many times but don't use the waxed variety.
- Don't panic if the appliqué paper sticks to the baking paper – it peels off easily.

Butterfly & floral canvas shoes

There is virtually nothing that can't be decorated with serviettes – including shoes! This project is definitely not for beginners so if you've never worked with serviettes before, turn to another project first and familiarise yourself with the technique before you tackle a pair of canvas shoes. Because of their shape a lot of patience and care is needed when decorating canvas shoes with serviette decoupage – we assure you that we had a few disasters before we got it right. We had to experiment extensively on these shoes because, let's face it, they take a little more battering than a pillowcase or apron. But don't be put off by the fact that we've told you it's a difficult project – it certainly is worth the effort and the decorated shoes are very popular. Nautical images also work for canvas shoes.

YOU WILL NEED
2 serviettes (plus a few extra
    for mishaps)
Canvas shoes
Methylated spirits/white
    vinegar
Cloth
Textile medium
White fabric glue
Water-based polyurethane
    varnish – matt
Flat, soft synthetic brush
Scissors
Craft knife

1 Clean the shoes with spirits to remove sizing which can prevent the serviette from sticking properly. Working on one shoe at a time, stuff it with plastic or paper so that it doesn't collapse when you work on it. Apply a coat of textile medium to the entire shoe.

2 While the medium on the shoe is still wet, lightly drape an entire (separated) serviette over the shoe and begin applying more medium over the serviette, working from the front backwards. Once you have completed the 'toe area', cut open the serviette down the centre, from the back up to (and including) the front section where the laces go. The serviette is now divided in two in order for you to work around each side of the shoe.

3 Continue applying the serviette around one side, ensuring that you mould it onto and around the stitching. Apply it directly over the lace holes as the excess will be cut away later. In order to make application of the serviette easier, it's a good idea to cut away excess paper as you work – don't try to cut it to size though, it will be trimmed when dry. Cutting slits into the excess serviette when you take it around curved areas also helps.

4 Once you get to the back seam of the shoe, carefully tear away the excess paper and begin working on the other side, once again from front to back. Tear away the excess at the back seam again so that the two pieces of serviette overlap slightly. By tearing the serviette, rather than cut-

ting it, the edges blend better. Once dry, use a hair dryer to heat-seal the medium.

5 Trim away excess paper from around the lace holes and the bottom of the shoe with a craft knife, making sure that you don't cut through the rubber or canvas. Now you can either cut away the excess paper from around the top of the shoe or you can apply more medium and mould it over the edge, trimming away any excess when it's dry.

6 Once dry, apply a coat of fabric glue to the entire decorated area, paying special attention to the edges in order to glue them down firmly. Clean away excess glue and leave to

dry. The shoe may feel slightly sticky when dry but don't worry, this will be eliminated with the next step.

7 Apply a final coat of polyurethane varnish to the area that you've worked on and leave to dry.

Retro jewellery box

This 'sixties-style' serviette is perfect for making items for a teenage girl's room. We discovered this after the jewellery box was claimed by our resident teenager even before it was finished. Her seven-year old sister wasn't too impressed but we managed to convince her that a mirror was much more useful than a jewellery box. So don't ignore these types of serviettes – they certainly have their place and their uses. Because of the nature of the design it's pointless cutting out images (apart from the little images put on the mirror) so we decided to cover the box using the entire serviette.

YOU WILL NEED
Wooden jewellery box
5 sixties-design serviettes
  – separated
Broken white PVA acrylic paint
Lavender acrylic craft paint
Foam applicator
Water-based polyurethane
  varnish
Embroidery scissors
Craft knife
Podge

1 Undo the screws from the hinges and separate the lid from the base of the box if possible. It's a lot easier to work on any decoupage item if you can do this.

2 Prepare the box according to the instructions for preparation of wood on page 23. Apply another 3 coats of broken white PVA to the areas that will be covered with the serviettes. This is to ensure that you will be applying them over an even, light background. When dry, seal this area with Podge.

3 Apply the top layer of the first serviette to the top of the box lid by dabbing down on it with a foam applicator that's been dipped in polyurethane varnish. Work from one side to the other, making sure that you have left yourself enough excess paper to tuck around and under the sides of the lid. Continue working over and down the sides of the box. Use scissors to trim away the excess paper on the corners as you get to them. Leave to dry.

4 Once dry, tuck the excess bits of paper underneath the lip of the box and 'glue' down in the same way, cutting away the extra paper on the corners. Then, when it's dry, trim away all excess paper with a craft knife.

5 Take a second serviette (which will be placed on the front of the base of the box) and match the design to the lid. Apply it in the same way. Leave to dry and trim. Continue working around the sides of the box, matching the pattern as you go.

6 When the box is completely covered and trimmed, paint the inside with 2-3 coats of lavender paint, allowing drying time between coats. Seal the entire box, inside and out with 3-4 coats of polyurethane varnish to complete.

Mirror
The hand mirror was painted with the lavender paint used inside the jewellery box. The images were first applied to paper so that they wouldn't disappear into the background. In order to do this, cut out the image and apply it to plain

white paper by brushing varnish over it using a soft, synthetic brush. Leave to dry before cutting it out and applying it to the frame. Use paper glue to stick the images because the normal way of applying serviettes (by brushing medium over them) doesn't work when the images are thicker. Finish off with 3-4 coats of polyurethane varnish.

HANDY HINTS

- Leave the box separate (don't put the lid back on the base) for about four days to avoid the two sticking together in case they are not properly dry.
- We have matched the pattern coming down the front of the box and then going around the sides. If you prefer, you can match the lid to the base all the way around the box but then the sides won't match.
- If you mess lavender paint onto the area decorated with serviettes, simply wipe it away with a damp cloth before it dries.
- The feet of the jewellery box were covered in the same way and glued on using white wood glue once the box was completed.

Fish bowl

There is definitely a revival in decoupage under glass and it's so much easier to use serviettes instead of traditional paper motifs. One of the major drawbacks when painting glass has always been the fact that the paint can become scratched over time, thereby ruining the finish. This applies particularly to bowls because the underside is easily scratched when it's moved around. Various crafters have come up with solutions to this problem but they take a huge amount of time and patience – two things that most of us don't possess. We believe that we've come up with a much easier option than most, so when you follow our instructions and wonder, "what on earth is this for?" – now you'll know.

1 Clean the underside of the bowl with spirits. Pull the back layer of paper off the serviettes and put aside (you'll need them later). Cut out the motifs you're going to use and separate them so that you're only left with the top layer.

2 Decide where the motifs are to be placed and (working on the underside of the bowl) begin gluing them in place by brushing varnish over them, working from one side of the motif to the other. We placed the larger motifs first and then 'filled-in' with the small ones. Once everything is glued down and the edges secure, leave to dry.

3 Apply one coat of varnish to the entire underside of the bowl and leave to dry (this will seal the serviette motifs further to prevent paint from seeping through them). Using the foam applicator, apply 3-4 coats of paint to the entire underside of the bowl, allowing drying time between coats. The first couple of coats will appear streaky when viewed from the right side of the bowl. You need to continue applying coats until the paint looks even. Leave to dry.

4 You will now use the layers of serviette that you put aside when beginning your project. Tear off the straight edges (they will show up when used) and then tear the rest of the paper into strips. Lay the strips over the painted area and begin 'gluing' them down, one at a time, by dabbing and pressing over them using varnish and a foam applicator. You will get wrinkles but don't worry as this will become a feature. Continue applying the strips in this manner, slightly overlapping the pieces as you work around the bowl. Leave the excess pieces of paper hanging over the edges of the bowl – they'll be trimmed away later. Take a damp cloth and press gently over the entire area on which you have just worked. This will remove excess varnish and help to press out air bubbles. Leave to dry.

5 Trim away the excess paper from around the sides of the bowl using a craft knife. Apply 2 coats of white paint over the 'papered' area, allowing drying time between coats. Seal with 2 coats of varnish to complete.

YOU WILL NEED
Glass bowl
3 fish serviettes
Methylated spirits/white vinegar
Cloth
Scissors
Water-based polyurethane varnish
Flat, soft synthetic brush
White acrylic paint
Foam applicator
Craft knife

HANDY HINTS

- The completed bowl should not be immersed in water. The undecorated side (the top) can be washed but the underside should only be wiped with a damp cloth.
- You can leave out the strips of paper placed over the paint but these add a huge amount of protection to the paint and give an interesting look to the completed bowl.
- Any smudges or paint can be cleaned off the top of the bowl using spirits. Stubborn marks can be scraped off carefully using a sharp blade.
- Bear in mind that the colour of the glass will affect the final shade of your paint (and, to a lesser degree, the serviette motifs). The bowl we used had a greenish-blue hue to it therefore the white paint actually looks pale blue.
- If you want to overlap a serviette motif you will have to paint the back of the motif (after it has been sealed) before placing another motif behind it otherwise you will see one serviette through the other.

Tomato place mats & plant pot

These tomatoes came to life when placed on a crisp white background. We've found that textile medium works particularly well on thick, textured fabric and these place mats were no exception. The plant pot is a bisque one that was painted and, for some reason, ended up looking like porcelain once it was finished. It isn't porcelain though, so bear in mind that it would be better to put a container inside the bisque one to hold a plant if you don't want to eventually ruin the finish. If any of you are wondering what place mats and plant pots have got to do with each other (and why the plant pot has tomatoes in it) the answer is fairly simple: we thought they'd make a good photograph together. Other than that, they have nothing in common and, while we all have a few odd habits, we certainly don't advocate putting a plant pot full of tomatoes on the table every time you serve breakfast! But then again, why not?

YOU WILL NEED

Cotton place mats – washed and dried
Tomato serviette – cut and separated
Water-soluble fabric marker
Flat, soft synthetic brush
Foam applicator (optional)
Textile medium

Place mats

1 Lay the serviette in position on the place mat and make markings around it with the fabric marker. Remove the serviette and apply medium to the area where it is to be placed. Put the serviette back in position and begin applying it by brushing more medium over it with the synthetic brush. Work from the outer edge inwards because the serviette will stretch and you may end up with too much serviette and not enough place mat if you do it the other way.

2 Complete all the place mats in this way and leave to dry. When dry, ensure that all edges are stuck firmly – if not, reapply medium, leave to dry and heat seal by covering the image with a cotton cloth and ironing (on a dry cotton setting). Turn the mat over and iron on the reverse side as well. Remove any remaining fabric marker marks by dabbing water over them.

HANDY HINTS

- Ensure that you work the serviette into the grooves of the fabric – we find it helps to use a foam applicator as well as a brush to do this.
- Always make sure that you use a fair amount of textile medium when applying serviettes to fabric (particularly thick, porous fabric) – you are more likely to damage the serviette if you use too little than if you use too much!
- When applying serviettes to thick fabric, it isn't normally necessary to use plastic sheeting underneath because the medium doesn't seep through, but you can take this precaution if you don't want to take a chance.

Plant pot

1 Prepare the pot according to the instructions for preparation of ceramics on page 27. Apply 3-4 coats of white paint to the entire pot (inside and out) using the foam applicator, allowing drying time between coats. Seal with one coat of Podge and leave to dry.

2 Apply the image to the pot by brushing polyurethane varnish over the dry image using the synthetic brush. Work from one side of the image to the other and ensure that you have plenty of varnish on your brush. Once dry seal with 3-4 coats of water-based polyurethane varnish (or 2 coats of lacquer medium).

YOU WILL NEED
Ceramic (bisque) plant pot
White acrylic paint
Foam applicator
Podge
Tomato serviette – cut and
   separated
Flat, soft synthetic brush
Water-based polyurethane
   varnish or
Lacquer medium for serviettes

HANDY HINTS

- It's often easier to cut off thin stems and apply them separately because it can be difficult to control them when applying a fairly large image.
- If you apply images with lacquer medium, then continue using the same product to seal the item. The same applies to the polyurethane varnish.

Olive tablecloth

With the ever-increasing costs of buying a pretty tablecloth, you can now make one for less than half the price. If you have never attempted fabric painting before, don't make this your first project. We're not saying this because it is difficult – it's not – but it's simply a large area to work on and it would be far better to first familiarise yourself with painting techniques. Incidentally, a lot of our readers seem to think we always get things right first time and never experience problems. Boy, are they wrong! If ever there was a jinxed project, this was it. On our first attempt we washed the fabric too soon after applying the second coat of paint and it cracked, so we had to give it to the dog as a basket liner. For our second attempt we somehow used the wrong kind of paint and the images sort of floated off when we washed it. We took that one out into the garden and hit it with shovels until we felt better! The lesson we learned is that you can't hurry fabric painting, especially when working on a large surface.

HANDY HINTS

- When painting fabric, be generous with the amount of paint you use – don't skimp unless you prefer a 'washed' look.
- When painting the border, avoid brushing paint towards the masking tape. Always paint away from it to prevent paint from seeping underneath.
- If you want to cut out intricate images such as the olives it's a good idea to iron them onto appliqué paper first because it strengthens them, thereby making cutting a lot easier.
- To tear around an image, such as the words, apply a little water around the section you want using a small artist's paintbrush – it makes it a lot easier to control the tear.

YOU WILL NEED

Calico – cut to size
4 olive design serviettes
Ivory fabric paint
Dark green fabric paint
Plastic sheet
Ruler
Fabric marker
High-density sponge
Foam applicator
Masking tape
Textile medium
Flat, soft synthetic brush
Magic appliqué paper
Baking paper
Cutting mat
Craft knife
Scissors

1 Wash, iron and hem the tablecloth before you start painting. Lay it down on a smooth surface (placing plastic underneath it to protect the surface you're working on) and stick it down with masking tape to make painting easier. Use a ruler to measure and mark a border around the outside of the cloth. Use the markings as a guide to apply masking tape to create straight lines for the border. Press the tape firmly into position.

2 Using the ivory paint, begin painting the central, cream area of the cloth. It's best to use a high-density sponge for a large area like this. Work from one side of the cloth to the other, remembering to keep a wet edge and blend the paint as you go along to avoid streaks. Leave the cloth to dry (properly!) for about 24 hours and decide if a second coat is necessary. If so, repeat this step and leave to dry. Remove the masking tape and heat seal by ironing (dry cotton setting) on the reverse side of the fabric.

3 Reapply the masking tape before beginning to paint the border. (remember to place the tape over the ivory paint and line it up with the existing markings otherwise you will end up with an unpainted area once you remove the tape). Use a sponge applicator to apply the dark green paint to the border, once again keeping a wet edge and blending as you work. Leave to dry, remove the tape and heat seal.

4 Roughly cut around the olive images (not the wording) on the serviettes and separate the layers as only the top one is used. Place the image onto the rough side of the appliqué paper (printed side facing up) cover with baking paper and iron on a dry cotton setting. Remove the baking paper and cut out the olives, using a craft knife for the intricate bits.

5 In order to prepare the words for application, simply tear around them (using the 'wet-and-tear method', see page 30) and separate the layers.

6 Lay the cloth on a flat surface and arrange the images. You can mark their position with a soft pencil but remember to rub out all pencil marks before applying the images. The olive images should be applied one at a time. In order to do this, remove the appliqué paper backing, place it in position (right side up), cover with baking paper and iron onto the fabric, using a dry cotton setting.

7 Once all the olive images are ironed on, you can begin applying the words. To do this, apply medium to the area where the words will be placed, lay the words over the medium and begin brushing down lightly using extra medium. Apply a liberal amount of medium over the olive images as well, ensuring that you extend it over the edges to prevent them from lifting. Leave to dry.

8 Heat seal all the images by covering them with either baking paper or a cloth and ironing over them (dry cotton setting again!). Keep the iron moving in order to prevent scorching the images. Iron on the reverse side as well to ensure that they are properly sealed.

Wine bottles wine holder

The only confusing thing about this project is the heading we've given it! The wine holder is a bisque pottery one that was a bit battered and chipped in places so we decided to give it a paint finish to artfully enhance the flaws (actually, neither of us felt like filling them). The serviette image was elevated using clay to give the bottles a three-dimensional look. This kind of technique is really quite easy to do and adds a new dimension to your work – no pun intended. Wine holders (or coolers) such as these are normally soaked in cold water to keep the wine cool. Unfortunately the finish will eventually be ruined if you do this, so we suggest that you avoid water at all costs once you've decorated your wine cooler.

YOU WILL NEED

Bisque wine holder/cooler

1 wine bottles serviette –
  cut & separated

Broken white PVA acrylic paint

Foam applicator

2 small paintbrushes

Yellow ochre artist's acrylic paint

Burnt umber artist's acrylic paint

Raw umber artist's acrylic paint

Podge

White air-hardening
  modelling clay

Plastic cling wrap

Rolling pin

Flat, soft synthetic brush

Water-based polyurethane varnish

Craft knife

Cutting mat

White wood glue

Paper moulding tool or nail
  cuticle set

Watercolour paint set

Fine artist's paint brush

1 Apply 2 coats of broken white paint to the wine holder and leave to dry. Make up a wash by mixing 1 part yellow ochre paint with 3 parts water. Apply the wash to the holder with a paintbrush, leave for a few minutes and then, using the dry brush, brush it out to blend it. This must be done before the paint begins to dry too much. Leave to dry fully.

2 Repeat the above process, using first the burnt umber and then the raw umber paint, remembering to give each wash time to dry before applying the next one. Once you're happy with the finish, seal with a coat of Podge and leave to dry.

3 Place a piece of clay between two sheets of cling wrap and roll it out (like pastry) until it's about 4 mm thick. Remove the top sheet of cling wrap and place the serviette motif onto the clay. Once it's in position, glue it down by brushing varnish over the serviette, working from one side to the other and extending the varnish slightly beyond the image to ensure good adhesion. Allow the varnish to dry, but not the clay.

4 Remove the piece of clay with the motif on it from the cling wrap and cut it out using a craft knife. If the clay is still too soft to work with leave it for a while and come back to it. When it has been cut out, use the moulding tool to neaten and smooth the edges – it helps if you keep dipping the tool in water as you work.

5 Apply white wood glue to the underside of the clay image and press it gently into position on and around the wine holder, squeezing out the excess glue from underneath as you do so. Clean away the glue from the sides and use the moulding tool to fix up any areas that may have become damaged in the gluing process. Lie the wine holder down and prop it up at the sides with towels to prevent it from rolling over. It's very important to keep the image flat, facing upwards while it is drying, otherwise the weight of the clay will cause the image to shift and slide.

6 Once the glue is dry, you can use your tool to mould the serviette image. Press fairly firmly but be careful not to damage the serviette. Once you're happy with your work, you can paint the edges of the clay using a fine paintbrush and the watercolour paints. Leave to dry and then seal with 2-3 coats of water-based polyurethane varnish.

Rose chair

This was a rather unattractive chair that had been sitting in Deborah's shed for about three years. Of course, as soon as we said we we're going to paint it, Christopher started going on about how it was sacrilegious to paint a yellowwood chair. It was only when we asked him for the money to buy a pine one instead that he decided to keep quiet – he's so cheap! The 'shed chair' now has pride of place in our daughter's bedroom instead of gathering dust so we don't think we did a bad thing. Because the chair was old and battered we decided that it needed a slightly rustic look, which is why we painted and decorated it to look like something granny may have had in her bedroom for many years. We inadvertently stumbled across the perfect paint to use when doing this technique, which has encouraged us both to look around for other bits of furniture that can be decorated in the same way because it is so easy.

You will need
Old chair
3 rose serviettes
400-grit sandpaper
600-grit sandpaper
Universal undercoat
White water-based ceiling paint
Paintbrush
Embroidery scissors
Flat, soft synthetic brush
Water-based polyurethane varnish
Podge

1 Prepare the chair according to the instructions for preparation of old wood on page 24. Ensure that you clean off any sawdust before applying a coat of universal undercoat to the entire chair. Leave to dry for 24 hours.

2 Apply 2 coats of white ceiling paint to the chair, allowing drying time between coats. We applied the paint fairly roughly in order to achieve a rustic look but if you prefer a smoother, denser paint coverage then apply it thinner and add another coat. Leave to dry.

3 Use 400-grit sandpaper to sand the edges of the chair where natural wear would take place. To achieve this look you need to sand right through the paint and down to the wood. Once you're happy with the look, give the whole chair a light sanding with 600-grit sandpaper, dust off and seal with a coat of Podge. Leave to dry.

4 Cut out the serviette images using embroidery scissors. In some cases it will be difficult to cut the intricate pieces because they could tear off – in this case simply cut around them as closely as possible (they have a white background which will blend into the white of the chair so this will not be noticeable). Separate the serviette layers (2 pieces of blue tac are really handy here) until you are left with only the top layer.

5 Place the images in position and glue them down, one at a time, by brushing the varnish over them. Work from one side of the image to the other and be sure to extend the varnish slightly beyond the edges of the image to ensure good adhesion. When the varnish has dried, lightly sand over the images with 600-grit sandpaper to give them a slightly distressed look, taking care not to sand them right off! Dust the chair off and seal with two coats of the polyurethane varnish to complete.

HANDY HINTS

- The ceiling paint sands beautifully because it is purely water-based. If you want to buy some, it's the 'one coat' variety available in most hardware stores.
- If your chair has any holes that need to be filled, do so before applying the undercoat.
- We used a flat, synthetic brush to apply the finishing coats of varnish because it doesn't soak up much varnish (so you don't use too much) and it gives a nice smooth finish.
- In some cases (on the opposite corners of the chair's seat) the rose images were turned over and applied in reverse in order to create a mirror image to balance the design. This is possible with serviettes because they are so transparent.

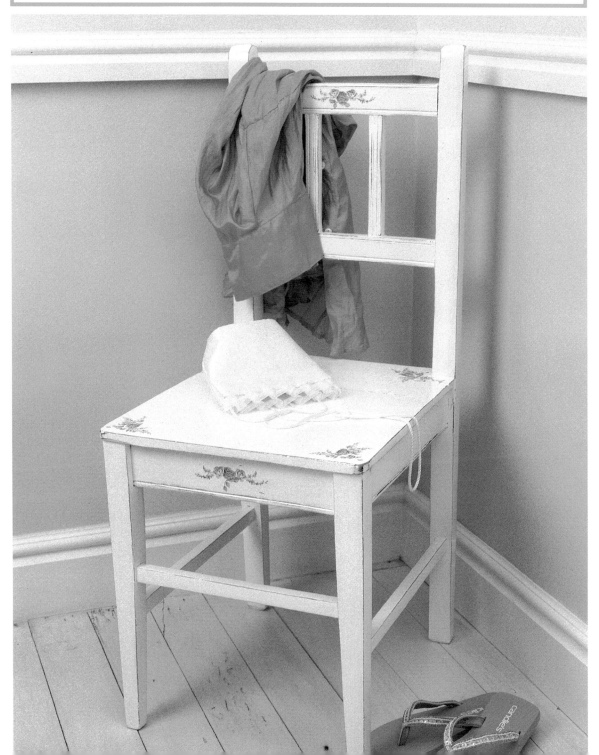

Elephant plate

Anybody who bought our last book will recognise the elephant image. We feel that he's so special that he deserves to be featured again, this time on a plate. Some of you may also remember that Tracy's husband, Geoff, felt there simply wasn't enough gold in our last book, so this project should make him happy. We used metal leaf because it's so much cheaper and easier to work with than true gold leaf. The only real problem that we experienced was being unable to find proper water-based gold size. We eventually had to settle for the thicker gold size which we are both convinced is white wood glue (we've sniffed enough products in our time – no, not to get high! – to recognise that smell). If you should ever come across a water-based gold size that is white (with a very slight purplish hue to it) and thin (like milk) buy up all the stock because you might never find it again! Don't worry if you have to use the thick stuff though. It still works but it's just not as easy to work with and takes a lot longer to dry.

1 Clean the underside of the plate with spirits. Pull the back layer of paper off the serviette and put it aside for later use (you'll probably need another as well, it all depends on how large your plate is). Cut out the elephant and separate the final two layers so that you're only left with the top one.

2 Turn your plate over (from now on you'll only be working on the underside) and place the elephant in position. Use the synthetic brush to glue the image down by brushing varnish over it, working from one side to the other. When it's glued down (but not dry) place a damp kitchen wipe over the image and carefully roll over it with the roller. This will press out air bubbles and excess varnish. Wipe away the varnish from around the image and leave to dry.

3 Apply one coat of gold size to the plate (including over the image). Work as neatly as possible because 'lumpy' streaks of size will be noticeable even when dry. Leave the size to become 'tacky' – anything from 20 minutes to 2 hours depending on the product and the weather. Ensure that the glue is transparent, with no 'white bits' showing before you begin applying the metal leaf.

4 Dust your fingers with talcum powder to make it easier to handle the metal leaf. Begin applying it by lying pieces down over the size. Once the leaf has settled on the size it cannot be repositioned so don't even try. When the entire underside of the plate is covered, take a soft cloth and press firmly on the gold or metal leaf to ensure that it's well stuck. Leave the plate (with all the loose, excess bits of metal leaf) overnight to dry properly.

5 Use a soft cloth to gently rub off the excess pieces of leaf. If you accidentally rub off a big piece, simply reapply metal leaf following the instructions above. Don't worry about little areas where the metal leaf has come off – it adds to the aged look of the plate.

6 Use a paintbrush to apply 2 coats of burgundy paint over the gold leaf, allowing drying time between coats. Take the layer (or layers) of serviette that you put aside when beginning the project, tear off the straight edges (which will show up if used) and then tear the rest of the paper into strips. Lay the strips over the painted area and begin gluing them down with varnish, one at a time, by dabbing and pressing over them with a foam applicator. Continue applying the strips in this manner, slightly overlapping the pieces as you work around the plate. Don't worry about strips of serviette paper hanging over the sides of the plate. Take a damp cloth and press gently over the entire area that you've just worked in order to remove excess varnish and bubbles. Allow to dry.

7 Trim away the excess paper from around the sides of the plate using a craft knife. Apply 2 coats of burgundy paint over the papered area, allowing drying time between coats. Seal with 2 coats of varnish to complete.

YOU WILL NEED

Glass plate
Elephant serviette
Methylated spirits/vinegar
Kitchen wipes
Manicure scissors
Water-based polyurethane varnish
Flat, soft synthetic brush
Rubber roller
Water-based gold size
Gold metal leaf
Talcum powder
Soft cloth
Paint brush
Burgundy acrylic paint
Foam applicator
Craft knife

HANDY HINTS

- It's a good idea to use a roller when applying a large serviette image under glass. By using a roller you can ensure that there will not be any 'shiny bits' showing up once the varnish has dried. These shiny areas are caused by air being trapped between the glass and the serviette image.
- Always use more, rather than less, varnish when applying serviettes to glass. This helps to alleviate the 'shiny bits' problem and any excess varnish can be cleaned away afterwards.
- Keep windows closed when working with metal leaf – it is flimsy and the slightest draught will send it flying around the room.
- If your plate (like ours) has indentations on it, be sure to press the leaf firmly into and around the raised areas before beginning to paint.

African books

We wanted to include something traditionally 'African' in our book (we live here after all) and this is it. These types of books are popping up all over the place in various gift shops, so why not make your own? They are quick and easy to make, can be personalised and, because virtually anyone can make use of a book, make lovely gifts. The serviette we used had so many images to choose from that it almost took longer to select a picture than it did to finish the project. We decided to use a neutral coloured handmade paper to cover the books before applying the serviette images because it works well with the colours of the card and the images.

1 If the book has a dark cover, apply a coat of cream paint to the outside cover (and spine) to prevent the colour showing through the handmade paper. Leave to dry.

2 Lay the open book on the paper and cut it to size, adding approximately 20 mm around the edges so that it can be folded over. Apply a fair amount of wood glue to the outside cover of the book and begin gluing the paper down. It's best to work from the front first (keeping the book closed) then bring the paper around the spine and over to the back. Use a roller to press the paper down and squeeze out excess glue.

3 Open the book in order to fold and glue down the edges of the paper. Cut away the paper that overlaps the spine because you won't be able to fold it over. Diagonally cut off the corners as well (about 5 mm from the edge) so that they won't end up too 'lumpy'. Apply glue to the handmade paper this time and glue the sides down, pulling the paper firmly over the edges and pressing down with your fingers, smoothing out any creases as you work.

4 In order to give your book a professional look, inside as well as out, cut the first and last pages of the book down a little – about 5 mm around the edges will do it – and glue them down over the entire inside cover.

5 Tear the lighter card to size and glue the serviette image onto it by brushing polyurethane varnish over it, working from one side to the other. Extend the varnish to all edges of the torn paper so that you don't end up with a shiny section in the centre. Leave to dry.

6 Tear a slightly bigger piece of darker card and glue to the front cover of the book using white wood glue. Take the smaller piece with the image on it and glue it down on top of the darker card. Leave to dry.

You WILL NEED
Hardcover exercise book/s
Handmade paper
Scissors
African serviette –
   cut & separated
Cream or white acrylic paint
Foam applicator
White wood glue
Rubber roller
Thin brown card (2 shades)
Water-based polyurethane
   varnish – matt
Flat, soft synthetic brush

HANDY HINTS

- If the wet paint seems to lift the spine binding slightly, don't worry: the glue and paper will sort out this problem.
- We chose handmade paper but any other kind of fancy paper also looks good, provided it doesn't overpower the serviette image.
- If your book has a margin, be sure to check that you are gluing the image on the front cover, otherwise the margin will end up on the wrong side – like our first attempt did!
- Once dry, it is a good idea to place the book between heavy books (or under a mattress) for a few days in order to flatten it back to its original shape.
- Make a matching pen and pencil bag from calico and decorate it with images from the same serviette for a really special gift.

Butterfly tea set

Transform a very ordinary, inexpensive tea set into one that looks like an expensive, hand-painted one. Decoupaging onto porcelain is ideal for people who want to produce something beautiful in a hurry. When working with butterflies, remember that they can be placed in any position – it's one of the few times when an image placed upside down doesn't look wrong. We know it's a bit daunting to cut butterfly antennae and many people are tempted to cut them off but try not to fall into this trap because it's obvious that there's something missing (and its also one of our pet hates).

1 Clean the tea set with spirits and leave to dry. Place a serviette image in position on the porcelain and hold it there with one hand. With the other hand begin applying the porcelain medium by brushing it onto the serviette from one side to the other, ensuring that your brush is always fairly wet. A light brush stroke is needed to avoid tearing the serviette. Extend the medium slightly beyond the image.

2 Wipe away any excess medium from around the image with a soft cloth dampened with spirits, taking care not to disturb the image in the process otherwise it will lift.

3 Continue applying the images to the rest of the tea set in this way, cleaning around them as you work. One small tip here: if you can't work around the porcelain without touching the still-wet images, rather let them dry before continuing. When you've finished, leave the porcelain to dry for 4 hours.

4 Preheat the oven to a temperature of 170 °C and bake the porcelain items for 30 minutes. Carefully take them out and leave to cool down. The baking almost 'melts' the images onto the porcelain.

YOU WILL NEED
White porcelain tea set
Methylated spirits/vinegar
2 butterfly serviettes – cut and separated
Soft cloth
Porcelain medium
Flat, soft synthetic brush

HANDY HINTS

- The tea set can be washed in lukewarm water but is not dishwasher safe.
- Porcelain must be baked in a conventional oven – not a microwave.
- Any dry excess medium that you have missed while cleaning around the butterflies can be scratched away carefully with a craft knife before you bake the porcelain.
- If the sides of the cut-out lift, simply reapply medium and re-bake.
- The colours on the serviette will darken slightly after being baked. This is not really noticeable with darker colours but whites end up looking as if they have been antiqued.

Chinese lamp & Zen garden

This project is dedicated to all the minimalists (or as one of our students once said after her third attempt to say, "minimalist" came out wrong: "people-who-don't-like-much-stuff-in-their-houses") and is a perfect example of 'less is more'. The lamp is a paper-covered one that we spotted in a lighting shop and we immediately thought it would be perfect with the Chinese serviette.

You can buy undecorated Zen garden sets at most craft shops that specialise in wooden blanks or you could try to persuade someone to make one for you (though we're not too sure how easy it is to make a rake). If you have an undecorated Zen garden-set lying around and you would like to give it a face-lift, simply sand it down to 'key' the surface before you begin painting.

YOU WILL NEED
Paper-covered lamp
Chinese serviette –
  cut & separated
Podge
Ruler
Pencil
Flat, soft synthetic brush
Water-based polyurethane
  varnish

YOU WILL NEED
Zen garden-set (with rake)
Chinese serviette -
  cut & separated
Black acrylic craft paint
Foam applicator
Podge
White air-hardening clay
Plastic cling wrap
Flat, synthetic brush
Water-based polyurethane
  varnish
Craft knife
Rubber roller or rolling pin
White wood glue
Fine artist's brush

Lamp

1 Apply a coat of Podge to the entire shade in order to protect the paper from marking while you're working on it. It's also easier to work on a surface that has been sealed because it is not so porous. Leave to dry.

2 Lay the lamp down so that the area you are going to work on is facing upwards. Use a ruler to find the middle of this area and make soft pencil markings so that you know where to position the serviette images.

3 Place the first image in position and glue it down by brushing polyurethane varnish down the middle of it and then working over to each side in turn. Extend the medium slightly beyond the image onto the shade. Apply the second motif in the same way and leave to dry. Seal the entire lampshade with a coat of water-based polyurethane varnish to complete.

Zen garden

1 Prepare the wood according to the instructions for new wood on page 23. Apply 2-3 coats of black paint to the entire Zen garden-box, inside and out, allowing drying time between coats. Seal the entire box with a coat of Podge.

2 Place a small piece of clay between two pieces of cling wrap and roll it out (like pastry) until it is about 5 mm thick. Remove the top sheet of cling wrap and place the serviette motif onto the clay. Once it is in position, glue it down by brushing varnish over the serviette, working from one side to the other and extending the varnish slightly beyond the image to ensure good adhesion. Leave to dry.

3 Remove the bottom layer of cling wrap, apply white wood glue to the underside of the clay image and press it gently into position on the front of the Zen garden, squeezing out the excess glue from underneath

as you do so. Clean away the glue from the sides and use your fingers or a toothpick dipped in water to fix up any areas that may have become damaged in the gluing process. Prop the Zen garden-box so that the image is facing upwards and leave it to dry. This prevents the weight of the clay from causing the image to shift and slide down.

4 When dry use the black paint and artist's brush to paint around the white edges of the clay and leave to dry. Apply 2 coats of polyurethane varnish to the entire Zen garden-box to complete.

5 The rake was covered with thin strips of serviette that were brushed directly onto the unpainted wood using polyurethane varnish and the synthetic brush. Apply the strips in sections, wait for them to dry, trim away excess paper and continue until the whole rake is covered.

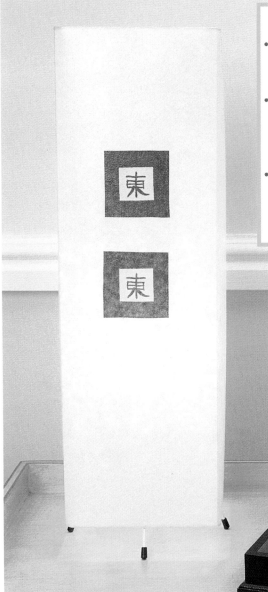

HANDY HINTS

- When applying images to the lamp, ensure that they line up with each other. If they don't you will notice it when you stand back and look at the lamp.
- If you make a mistake and things look a little wonky once glued down, remove the cut-out before the varnish dries otherwise you won't be able to remove it without damaging the paper on the lamp.
- Don't put sand in the Zen garden-box for at least 24 hours after varnishing. The varnish needs time to dry completely and you could end up damaging the finish if you are too enthusiastic.

Strawberry picnic basket

This picnic basket looked so pretty once it was finished that we felt an immediate and powerfully seductive urge to fill it with food and wine, take the rest of the day off and go out to the lagoon. Unfortunately, our deadline (and almost continuous rain) prevented us from giving in to our decadent urges but the basket is still there and we've promised ourselves it won't be long before we can use it. Serviettes are perfect for decorating onto wicker because they mould over it so easily. Don't just limit yourself to picnic baskets: you can find a huge variety of wicker bathroom, bedroom and even kitchen accessories that can be decorated using this same technique.

1 Using the small flat paintbrush, apply 3 coats of white acrylic paint to the outside of the basket, allowing drying time between coats. Apply a coat of varnish (using the foam applicator) to the painted surface. Leave to dry.

2 Arrange the serviette motifs onto the basket before you begin gluing. A little blue tac placed on the back of the images – before you separate the final two layers – will help to keep them in position. If necessary, cut away some of the foliage in order to make the design work.

3 Lay the basket on its side in order to begin applying the motifs. Remember to remove the blue tac and final layer of paper from the back. Glue down one image at a time by brushing polyurethane varnish over it using the synthetic brush. Work from one side to the other, moulding the serviette around the wicker and extending the varnish slightly beyond the image so that it doesn't lift.

4 Glue down the next image in the same way, making sure that the foliage of the two images are placed next to each other. Carry on gluing (sounds like the name of a movie, doesn't it?) until you have completed one side of the basket. Leave to dry before continuing, otherwise you could damage the wet images when you turn the basket.

5 Continue in this way until all four sides have been decorated. When dry apply 3 coats of varnish to the entire basket, allowing drying time between coats.

You will need

Unvarnished wicker basket
2 strawberry serviettes – images cut out but not separated
White acrylic paint
Small flat paintbrush
Foam applicator
Water-based polyurethane varnish
Flat, soft synthetic brush
Blue tac/prestik

HANDY HINTS

- Be careful when working next to a motif that is still wet – it could tear or lift if you touch it.
- If the undecorated basket is a little rough, it can be sanded with 400-grit sandpaper before you begin painting.
- If you are battling to apply the images, try gluing down the strawberries first and then the foliage.
- If you are a sucker for punishment you can paint the inside of the basket as well. If not, simply paint the inside lid.

Flower tray-cloth & tea cosy

Some time ago we gave a demonstration on serviette decoupage to a whole bunch of ladies from our local embroidery guild. One of the questions that came up was whether serviette decoupage on fabric could be used in conjunction with embroidery. We had never connected the two crafts before but after giving it a little thought we answered, "we don't see why not" and decided to try it for ourselves. The only drawback to this was that while one of us can sew, neither of us had actually attempted any embroidery since Grade 4. Luckily, our publisher had just brought out a wonderful book on embroidery (FUNKY STITCHES by Anita Plant) and, being two of her most loyal supporters, we bought a copy and taught ourselves a few basic stitches. We can now, without a shadow of a doubt, state than you can definitely combine the two crafts and the results are exceptionally satisfying.

YOU WILL NEED
White cotton tray cloth & tea cosy
Flower serviette – cut & separated
Water-soluble fabric marker
Plastic
Textile medium
Flat, soft synthetic brush
Embroidery thread (2 colours)
Embroidery needle

1 Wash and iron the fabric before beginning to work on it to remove any sizing. Decide where the serviette motifs are to be placed and make small markings on the fabric around each one with a fabric marker. Lay plastic under the fabric to protect your work surface. Remove the motifs (one at a time) and apply medium to the area where the motif will be placed. Lay the serviette over the wet area and begin gluing it down by brushing more medium over the motif, working from one side to the other.

2 Continue applying the motifs in this way until they are all glued down. Leave to dry and remove the fabric marker markings with a little water and a cloth. Heat seal by covering the decorated areas with fabric and ironing on a dry cotton setting. Turn the items over and iron on the back as well.

3 We decided to use french knots for the centre of the flowers. This stitch is done as follows (FUNKY STITCHES, page 92): Bring the needle through to the front of the centre of the flower where the knot or knots are to be placed. Use your left hand to hold the thread taut and wind the thread around your needle, once for a small knot or twice for a bigger one. Turn the needle round and insert it next to where the thread first came out, still holding the thread taut. Pull the needle through, releasing the thread at the last minute. Fill the centre of the flowers with french knots – it looks better if you don't follow any set pattern when doing them.

- Unless you are a superb and neat embroiderer (is there such a word?) and the back of your work is as neat as the front, we suggest that you decorate and sew the fabric before making up the tray cloth and tea cosy. In that way you can hide any scruffy work with lining and no one will know that you can't sew to save your life!
- Wash the finished items by hand in lukewarm water and don't rub the motifs - you'll create a stone-washed effect on the serviette and you could damage the embroidery.
- There are many simple, attractive embroidery stitches that can be used in conjunction with serviettes and it's worth experimenting.

Herb coffee set

In this project you can see that it's also possible to use an entire serviette to cover porcelain items. Once again this is a quick and easy technique with the only challenge being to try and keep the lines of the serviette straight but even that doesn't take too much effort. You could decorate an entire dinner service in this manner but bear in mind that continued use of a knife and fork in the centre of the plate will eventually damage the serviette – it would be better to decorate the outer rim and leave the centre undecorated. We chose a serviette with fairly subtle, small images which could be cut in half without being noticeable – bear this in mind when using the technique.

1 Clean the porcelain with spirits and leave to dry. Use a ruler to measure the height of the cups and sugar bowl. Take off 8 mm from this measurement – serviettes stretch when applied and we also left an undecorated rim around the top and bottom of these items – and make light pencil markings on the serviette. Use a ruler and craft knife to cut the serviette to size.

2 When cutting the serviette for the cups, you will also have to measure the circumference of the cup because the serviette stops just short of the handle. The best way to do this is to wrap the serviette piece around it and make a mark where it needs to be cut. Once again, cut it smaller because of stretching. You don't have to be as precise with the sugar bowl because the serviette will overlap at the back and you can tear away the excess afterwards.

3 Separate the serviette layers – you need only the top one. Place the serviette in position, hold it in place and begin applying medium over it with the synthetic brush. Work from one side of the porcelain around to the other. Concentrate on keeping the edges straight as you work and don't worry about wrinkles: you can't avoid them so make them a feature. Extend the medium slightly beyond the serviette to prevent the edges from lifting.

4 When covering the sugar bowl, apply the serviette all the way around it until the edges overlap slightly. Tear away the excess paper (torn edges blend better) by holding down the wet serviette with your brush and carefully pulling the rest away. Cover the spoon by wrapping a small piece of serviette around the handle and tearing the edges where they overlap at the back.

5 In order to cover the plate cut a serviette to approximately the size of the plate. Place the serviette in position and begin applying medium from the centre and then work your way outwards. This is the only time that we advise applying serviettes in this way. Try not to stretch it too much in the centre because this only leads to uneven wrinkling around the edges. Leave the excess paper dangling over the sides until dry and then trim with a craft knife. Apply a little extra medium around the edges after you have trimmed to ensure they don't lift.

6 Leave the set to dry for about 4 hours. Preheat the oven to a temperature of 170 °C and bake the porcelain for 30 minutes. Take it out and leave it to cool down.

YOU WILL NEED
Porcelain cups, sugar bowl & plate
3 herb serviettes
Methylated spirits/vinegar
Pencil
Metal ruler
Craft knife
Cutting mat
Porcelain medium
Flat, soft synthetic brush

HANDY HINTS

- If the plate has too much uneven wrinkling on it, carefully lift the wet serviette up, reposition it and reapply medium – it will go on more evenly.
- Try not to touch the wet serviette when working around the porcelain otherwise you could damage it.
- If you are not happy with your work, simply wash the serviette off before baking and start again.

Garden birdhouse

This project was a complete diversion from our usual style of decoupage and ended up being a lot of fun to make. We'd had the garden serviette for some time and when we saw the birdhouse in a craft shop we knew the two would work well together. Some crackle mediums can only be sealed with oil-based products so always check the instructions. Try to use a medium that is compatible with water-based products because they are easier to work with and are non-yellowing.

YOU WILL NEED
Wooden birdhouse
Garden serviette –
    cut & separated
Yellow ochre acrylic paint
Podge
Foam applicator
Broken white PVA acrylic paint
Dark green acrylic paint
Crackle medium
Flat, soft synthetic brush
Water-based polyurethane
    varnish

1 Prepare the birdhouse according to the instructions for preparation of new wood on page 23. Use the applicator to apply 3 coats of yellow ochre to the sides and base of the birdhouse, allowing drying time between coats. Seal with a coat of Podge.

2 Paint the roof and eaves with 3 coats of broken white, allowing drying time between coats. This will be the colour that shows up through the cracks. When dry apply an even, horizontal coat of crackle medium over the roof and eaves. Leave to dry.

3 Working horizontally again, apply a coat of dark green paint over the crackle medium. Work evenly in one motion from one side to the other without stopping. Don't paint in the normal way, moving the applicator backwards and forwards, as there should be no overlapping of paint; overlapping will result in smudged cracks, which will ruin the effect.

4 Leave to dry for at least 2 hours without touching it. Cracks will start appearing almost immediately. When dry, seal with 4-6 coats of polyurethane varnish, allowing drying time between coats.

5 The roof is done, now for the rest of it. Glue the images down by brushing polyurethane varnish over them using the synthetic brush, working from one side of the image to the other. Leave to dry and apply 4-6 coats of varnish to the sides and base, allowing drying time between coats.

HANDY HINTS

- The dark green paint can be watered down slightly to make application easier but not too much otherwise the cracks will run.
- We tore around the intricate floral areas of the images instead of trying to cut them out (see 'wet-and-tear method' on page 30) . The background colour of the serviette is similar to the colour of the birdhouse so it's not noticeable. Torn edges always blend better than cut ones.
- If you make a bit of a mess with paint on the sides of the house while you're painting the roof, it can be easily cleaned with a damp cloth because Podge was applied for protection.
- We recommend applying at least 6 coats of varnish to any items that will be kept outdoors.
- If the crackle doesn't work the first time round, don't despair. Before the paint dries, wash it off with warm water and reapply crackle and paint.
- You can dry the crackle (after applying the green paint) with a hairdryer to speed up drying time.

Shell candles

Decoupaged candles are very pretty and don't take long to complete. We have made many candles like these for gift shops but had to give it up because we couldn't keep up with the demand and still write books. Always use thicker candles that burn down in the centre otherwise the serviette itself will start burning as well. The same serviette was used on both candles but the techniques differ. Serviettes work perfectly on candles because they mould so well to the curved surface. Candle medium can also be mixed with acrylic paint so that you can paint the candle before decorating it.

Covered candles

1 Clean the candle with spirits and leave to dry. Cut the serviette down to a workable size, ensuring that you leave it big enough to go around and under the candle. Keep the bits that you cut away because you can use them for the cracked candles. Separate the layers of the serviette; you only need the top one.

2 Begin applying the serviette by holding it in position and brushing candle medium over it using the synthetic brush. Work down the candle, moving around it until the two ends meet. Cut or tear away the excess paper and overlap the two edges slightly. Leave to dry.

3 Turn the candle upside down and, using the same method, glue the serviette down underneath. It's a good idea to snip away excess bits of paper before gluing it in order to avoid any lumpy bits underneath. Leave to dry and then apply another coat of medium to the entire candle.

Cracked candles

1 Wipe the candle with spirits and leave to dry. Use the applicator to apply crackle medium to the candle using even, vertical strokes. Leave to dry before painting on the light sand paint. Apply it in one motion, working from the top to the bottom of the candle. Don't paint backwards and forwards or overlap paint otherwise the cracks will smudge.

2 The cracks will start forming almost immediately but don't touch the candle. Leave it to dry for at least 2 hours and then apply a coat of varnish over the cracked area to protect it.

3 Cut out the shell motifs and separate the layers as only the top layer is used. Glue the shell motifs into position by brushing varnish over them using the synthetic brush. When dry apply another coat of varnish over the entire decorated candle for added protection.

You will need

Candles
Methylated spirits/vinegar
2 shell serviettes
Crackle medium
Light sand acrylic craft paint
Candle medium
Water-based polyurethane varnish
Foam applicator
Flat, soft synthetic brush
Embroidery scissors

HANDY HINTS

- The light sand-coloured paint can be watered down slightly to make application easier.
- It is a lot easier to work on a candle if you balance it on top of a jar that is just a little smaller than the candle. Leave it on the jar to dry too.
- Ensure that you use one of the crackle mediums that can be sealed with a water-based varnish. The instructions on the side will confirm if you have chosen the right one.

Infant T-shirt & bib

Serviette decoupage is not only restricted to items for the home. Now your children or your friends' children can also wear your decoupage. This is a perfect way to decorate plain, cheap items of clothing and turn them into something unique and special. Young children especially love clothing decorated with their favourite images and with the fantastic choice in serviettes available these days, you shouldn't have a problem finding something suitable. These bibs and T-shirts also make wonderful gifts. But don't even think about decorating T-shirts for teenagers – they're way too cool to wear anything made by Mom!

YOU WILL NEED
T-shirt
Towelling bib
Infant serviette – cut & separated
Water-soluble fabric marker
Plastic sheet
Textile medium
Flat, soft synthetic brush

1 Wash and iron the items before working on them. Place the serviette image on the T-shirt, make markings around it with the fabric marker and remove the image. Place a piece of plastic inside the T-shirt to prevent the textile medium from seeping through to the back. Apply the medium to the area you will be working on, taking it up to the markings. Lay the image back down over the wet area and begin gluing it down by brushing extra medium over it, using the synthetic brush. Work from one side of the image over to the other and extend the medium slightly beyond the edges to ensure good adhesion.

2 The bib can be decorated in the same way but a little more pressure is needed to mould the image into the thicker fabric. A good way to do this is to apply the image and then dab over it with the edge of the brush to push it into the towelling. Make sure that your brush is always wet (with medium) otherwise you could lift the serviette.

3 Leave to dry. Heat seal by covering with a thin cloth and ironing over the decorated image on a dry cotton setting. Iron on the reverse side of the image as well. The marks left behind from the fabric marker can be removed with water.

HANDY HINTS

- Try to find a good-quality, thicker T-shirt if at all possible. The really thin ones are likely to get a 'water-mark' around the edges of the image.
- Serviettes always work better on natural fabrics so try to use a pure cotton T-shirt or at least something without too much polyester.
- It's best to hand-wash fabric items decorated with serviettes and try not to rub over the image otherwise you will get a stone-washed effect, although this sometimes looks rather nice.
- If any edges of the image lift over time, simply reapply medium and heat seal.
- We shouldn't have to say this but we will anyway: don't iron the back of the bib if the bib is backed with plastic!

Apple cutting board

Glass cutting boards have become very popular so we decided to have a go and try out a new 'iron-on' technique. By decorating your own cutting board you can match it up to all the other decoupaged items in your kitchen. We've chosen to use an entire serviette to work with but you can also use cut out images. If you prefer to paint the background (so that the work surface will not be visible through the glass cutting board) you can do so. However, a word of warning: you won't be able to immerse the cutting board in water to clean it – you'll only be able to wipe it with a damp cloth. You will need to use armour-plated glass for the cutting board, which can be obtained from your local glazier.

The jam jars are cheap glass ones, which we covered completely.

You will need

Armour-plated glass – cut to the size of the serviette
Jam jars
2 apple serviettes – separated
Methylated spirits/vinegar
Porcelain medium
Foam applicator
Flat, soft synthetic brush
Soft cloth
Rubber roller
Craft knife

Cutting board

1 Clean the glass with spirits and leave to dry. Use a foam applicator to apply one even coat of porcelain medium to one side of the glass. Leave to dry. Place the serviette, printed side down, on the side with the medium. Carefully iron (dry cotton setting) over the serviette, working from one side to the other. The heat from the ironing bonds the serviette to the glass

2 Using the synthetic brush, apply a coat of porcelain medium over the serviette, once again working from one side to the other. Make sure that you have covered the entire area with medium and have not missed any spots. To check: lift the glass up, turn it over (no, don't put it down!) And hold it up to see if you have missed any bits.

3 Place a damp cloth over the serviette and roll out any air bubbles using the roller. When dry apply a second coat of medium and leave to dry. Use a craft knife to trim away any excess pieces of serviette from around the edges. Heat the oven to a temperature of 170 °C and bake for 30 minutes to seal.

Jam jars

1 Remove all the bits of plastic and metal and clean the outside of the glass with spirits. Cut the serviette down to a workable size, ensuring that it's big enough to go around the jar.

2 Begin applying the serviette by holding it in position and brushing medium over it using a synthetic brush. Work down the jar, moving around it until the two ends of the serviette meet. Cut or tear away the excess paper and overlap the two edges slightly. Leave to dry and use a craft knife to trim away the excess paper at the base and top of the jar. Cover the base and lid of the jar in the same way. Heat seal at 170 °C in a conventional oven like you would the cutting board.

Shoe boxes

Cardboard storage boxes
3 shoe serviettes – cut out but not
  separated
Broken white PVA acrylic paint
Sandy yellow acrylic craft paint
Acrylic scumble glaze
2 foam applicators
Podge
Blue tac/prestik
Flat, soft synthetic brush
Water-based polyurethane varnish

These cardboard storage boxes were bought from a homeware shop. There was nothing special about them apart from the fact that they're useful for storing all sorts of junk. By decorating them they serve two purposes: they are still useful for storage and they look really good, so can be displayed in the open rather than shoved away in the back of a cupboard. Other cardboard boxes (shoeboxes for instance) can be decorated in the same way provided that the cardboard isn't too thin otherwise it will warp when painted. We both loved the shoe serviette and the boxes seemed like the perfect place to use it.

1 Paint the box with 4 coats of broken white paint, allowing drying time between coats. Mix up a glaze as follows: 1 part sandy yellow, 2 parts scumble glaze and 3 parts water. Apply an even coat of the glaze to the lid of the box with a foam applicator. Use the other dry applicator and brush evenly over the glaze in one direction to smooth it out. Paint the base of the box in the same way and leave to dry.

2 Seal the painted area with a coat of Podge and allow to dry. Arrange the serviette motifs on the box – a little prestik will keep them in place. Before gluing, remove both the prestik and the last layer of paper from the back of the motif. Use the synthetic brush to apply polyurethane varnish over the images, working from one side to the other. Leave to dry.

3 Complete the project by applying 3-4 coats of polyurethane varnish over the entire decorated area, allowing sufficient drying time between coats.

HANDY HINTS

- Prop the box base and lid up on a book when applying the paint finish – it makes it a lot easier to manoeuvre them without smudging the finish.
- Don't touch the paint finish while it's still wet otherwise it will smudge and you won't be able to touch it up without it being noticeable.
- We used foam applicators for the paint finish because we wanted a streaky look. If you prefer a more subtle, blended finish use paintbrushes instead.
- If you accidentally get paint on the leather straps of the box, it can be cleaned off with a cloth dampened with methylated spirits.
- Because there are folds inside the box, painting would be difficult (not to mention boring) so we decided not to bother.

Butterfly bag & hat

We thought of decorating a bag after a number of people asked Tracy if she had decoupaged the rose-covered handbag that she was using at the time. We had this bag made for us and then decorated it for a fraction of the price of the original one. If you can't sew, it's time to make friends with someone who can – you could always offer to decorate items for your new friend in exchange for her services (oth-erwise you're going to have to pay her!). The hat was bought at a local clothing store and decorated using the same technique as the bag. As it is virtually impossible to cut out the intricate images on this serviette, we have torn around them instead. This is not noticeable once the serviette is applied because the background of the serviette and the bag are the same colour.

YOU WILL NEED

Cotton bag

2 butterfly serviettes – separated

Fine paintbrush

Water-soluble fabric marker

Plastic sheet

Textile medium

Flat, soft synthetic brush

Fabric paint sealer

1 It is best to work on one side of the bag at a time, so start with the front. You need to measure the width of this section and then tear the serviette to that size. The best way of doing this is to use the fine paintbrush to make small dabs of water right around the outside of the serviette image that you are going to use, and pull gently to tear the two sections apart (see page 30).

2 Lay the image in position and make markings around it with the fabric marker. Place a piece of plastic inside the bag to prevent medium from seeping through to the other side of the bag. Remove the image and apply medium to the section where the image will be placed, taking the medium up to the markings.

3 Apply the image over the wet area and begin brushing it down using the synthetic brush and more medium. Work from one side over to the other, ensuring that you always have a wet brush. If you have an excess piece of serviette when you get to the other side, carefully tear it away and brush the edges down. Allow to dry.

4 Continue decorating all four sides in this manner and leave to dry. Cover the decorated sections with a thin cloth and iron over them (dry cotton setting) in order to heat seal. Apply at least 2 coats of fabric paint sealer to the entire outside of the bag for added protection. Heat seal again.

HANDY HINTS

- It is difficult to apply large images without getting any wrinkles, so don't worry about them. You can use your fingers to smooth out many of them once you have applied the image but make sure that the image is wet with medium otherwise it will lift or tear.

- It's not necessary to try to match up the pattern around the sides of the bag. It's such a busy serviette that you won't notice if the front and sides don't match.
- We added butterflies to the bag to balance the design and prevent it from looking too stark.

Lavender watering can

We found this old galvanized steel watering can at our local florist shop where it had been dumped in a corner - it pays to scratch around in places like this. It was filthy and battered and we picked it up for next to nothing. Once we had cleaned it up though and pressed out most of the dents we were raring to go (well, one of us was anyway). A fair amount of work goes into decorating a watering can and we find that most people are loath to ruin it by letting anybody use it for something silly – like watering plants – in case it gets damaged. Therefore we don't recommend that you leave it exposed to the elements as it will spoil with time.

1 Prepare the watering can according to the instructions for preparation of galvanized steel on page 24. Use the applicator to paint 3 coats of pastel yellow to the inside and outside of the can, allowing drying time between coats.

2 Mix up a glaze as follows: 1 part white paint, 2 parts scumble glaze and 3 parts water. Apply an even coat of glaze to the outside of the watering can then, using the dry paintbrush, brush over it to smooth out the glaze. Once the glaze has dried, seal the entire can, inside and out with Podge. Leave to dry.

3 Place the serviette motif in position and hold it there with one hand. Apply the motif by brushing polyurethane varnish over it using the synthetic brush. Always use a fairly wet brush, work from one side to the other and extend the varnish slightly beyond the edges of the serviette. Leave to dry. Finish off by applying 4-6 coats of varnish, allowing drying time between coats.

YOU WILL NEED
Galvanized steel watering can
Lavender serviette –
   cut & separated
Foam applicator
Medium size paint brush
Pastel yellow acrylic craft paint
White acrylic craft paint
Acrylic scumble glaze
Podge
Flat, soft synthetic brush
Water-based polyurethane varnish

HANDY HINTS

- If the watering can is to be kept indoors, glue cork on the base to finish it off. However, if you intend keeping it outside, rather paint and varnish the base to make it more durable.
- Don't take short cuts with the preparation otherwise the paint will eventually peel off.
- If you want to use the watering can for its real purpose don't paint the inside.

Paper tole tea cups

Paper tole is the art of cutting, mounting and gluing multiple cut-outs of the same image onto a background. Clear silicon is used to glue the pieces into place, one on top of the other. You normally need at least five copies of the same image to complete a picture – which is why a pack of serviettes is ideal – although the images do need to be backed with paper to make them thicker before you can start working with them.

The most important thing with paper tole is to work out which parts of the image will be in the foreground and which will remain the background. Remember that you want to create a lifelike image and there is no right or wrong way, it is how you perceive the picture. The secret to good cutting is to 'over-cut' some sections. In other words, cut slightly beyond the outline (this is referred to as 'the natural cutting line') so that, when you lay the next piece, no cutting edges are visible underneath. This enables you to tuck one piece behind the other.

The only time that you would cut exactly on the natural cutting line is when it is not going to be overlapped by another part of the picture. Neither the first nor the final piece will be over-cut.

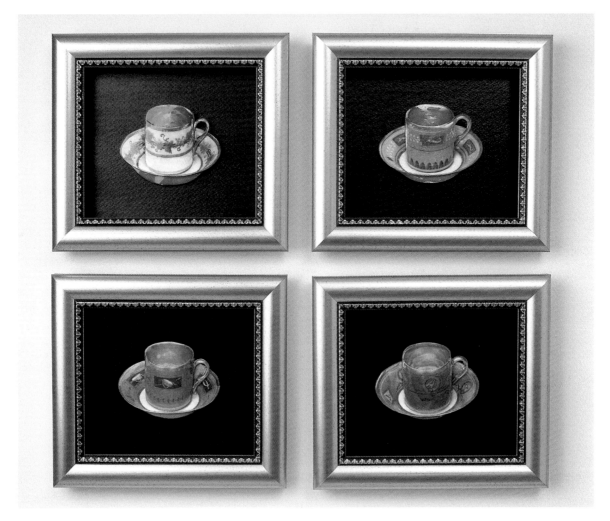

1 Use the applicator to seal the mounting board with 2 coats of Podge – this protects it from finger marks and spilt silicon. Roughly cut around the images, separate the layers of the serviette and then glue the top layer onto plain white paper. Do this by placing the images onto the white paper and brushing polyurethane varnish over them. Try to work from one side to the other and, for best results, use the synthetic brush. Leave to dry.

2 Have a pencil handy to label the back of the pieces you are going to cut so that you don't get confused. Cut out one entire teacup along the natural cutting line, which will be used as your base print and label it number 1. The next piece is the saucer. Don't cut around the cup because you don't want to see cutting lines – simply cut straight through it (you will end up with an oval shape). Label this piece number 2 and lay it down (right side up) in position on piece number 1. Continue working in this way, remembering to over-cut pieces that will be overlapped. Label them as you cut them out and place them in their correct position – a little like building a puzzle. The last piece (the front section of the cup) will be cut on the natural cutting line.

3 Paint all white edges of the pieces with watercolour paints. Leave to dry. Shape each piece before mounting to give them a more realistic effect. Do this by pulling them over a pencil to give them a slightly rounded look.

4 Take the first piece to be mounted (number 1) and squeeze out a small blob of silicon and scrape it off the top of the tube with a toothpick. Place the toothpick with the silicon down onto the back of the piece (about 3 mm from the edge) and gently roll the toothpick in your fingers. The silicon should remain in a round blob on the piece and you will be able to pull the toothpick free. Continue applying blobs of silicon all the way around the piece, including the centre.

5 Carefully pick up the piece and place it in position on the mounting board. Press ever so slightly so that it bonds to the board. Prepare and mount the rest of the pieces, making sure that they are all lined up properly on top of each other. Leave to dry overnight.

6 Varnish the picture with poster & watercolour varnish to give it a porcelain-like appearance. Apply it using a fabric painting bottle with a small nozzle. Working on one section at a time, make little dots of varnish next to each other which will then join together to give even coverage. Any bubbles can be pricked with a toothpick. Place the varnished picture on a flat surface in a dust-free environment to dry. Leave for four days before applying a second coat of varnish in the same way.

YOU WILL NEED

Black mounting board – cut to size
5 tea cup serviettes
3 sheets A4 white paper
Podge
Foam applicator
Flat, soft synthetic brush
Water-based polyurethane varnish
Embroidery scissors
Soft pencil
Watercolour set
Fine paintbrush
Tube of clear silicon
Toothpicks
Daler-rowney's poster & watercolour varnish
Fabric paint bottle

HANDY HINTS

- If you have 'double imagery' on the handle of the cup simply snip away the visible sections from underneath with embroidery scissors.
- Be careful not to lean on sections that have just been mounted – you will flatten them and ruin the effect.
- We covered this technique more extensively in ALL NEW DECOUPAGE so, if you would like more information, rush out immediately and get yourself a copy!
- For those people who have done this before using 3D packs, you'll find that serviettes will need a lot more silicon than you're used to – especially around the edges.

Rose chest of drawers

We decided to use a combination of two serviettes for this project. People usually tend to ignore serviettes that have no images on them, but they can be used to create texture, as we have done here. After choosing the rose serviette, we looked for a plain one that worked well with it and the silvery-grey choice was perfect. The project went fairly quickly and the only problem we had was trying to find small enough drawer knobs once it was finished. Bear this in mind when buying items to decorate: rather try to purchase something that already has hinges and handles because sometimes it's hard to get the right size. We eventually had to make our own knobs out of wooden beads. When decorating something like this, always remove the drawers before beginning to paint and wait at least 4 days after you have applied your final coat of varnish before replacing them to prevent them from sticking together.

YOU WILL NEED

Wooden chest of drawers

2 rose serviettes

3 silver/grey serviettes – separated

Light grey acrylic craft paint

Podge

Foam applicator

Scissors

Flat, soft synthetic brush

Water-based polyurethane varnish

Craft knife

1 Prepare the drawer set by following the instructions for preparation of new wood on page 23. Paint the outside of the chest (and drawers) with a coat of grey paint and leave to dry. If it doesn't cover well you will have to give it another coat. Don't worry if it's a little streaky because it's only a base on which you'll glue the serviettes. Paint the inside of the drawers properly (2-3 coats) and leave to dry. Seal the outside of the chest and both the inside and outside of the drawers with Podge and leave to dry.

2 Measure the front of the drawers and cut pieces of rose serviette accordingly – you don't have to be too precise because serviettes stretch when applied and the excess bits will be trimmed later. Apply these pieces to the drawers (don't forget to separate the layers first) by holding them down on the front of the drawer and then brush varnish over them. Use the synthetic brush and work from one side to the other. Don't worry about wrinkles as, strangely enough, we want them for this technique! Once the serviette is glued down (but still wet) dab over the entire decorated area with a dry applicator. This pushes out the excess varnish and air bubbles. Leave to dry.

3 Cut the silvery-grey serviette in half and place one entire half over the front of the chest. Glue it down to the drawer surrounds using the above method and leave to dry. Cut away the excess paper from the surrounds and drawer holes using a craft knife. Then trim off any excess paper from the drawers themselves. Decorate the rest of the chest in the same way, one side at a time. Finish off by applying 2 coats of varnish, allowing drying time between coats.

HANDY HINTS

- If your blade is inclined to slip and cut into the wood when trimming the excess paper from the sides, rather trim when the paper is still slightly wet because you don't have to use as much pressure.
- Our 'bead knobs' were filled with wood filler at one end, covered with a piece of serviette and screwed in place from the inside of the drawers. If you'd like to try this yourself make sure that the screws aren't too long otherwise they'll push the filler out and you'll have to start again.

Nautical wall hanging

What we had in mind here, when we asked a seamstress to make this up for us, was some sort of shoe holder that could hang behind a cupboard door. Our only instruction was that we didn't want it too small and that the rest was up to her. She made a very good job of it but got a little carried away: as you can see, the only door that this would ever fit behind is the one you open to drive the car into the garage! The tip we'd like to pass on to you is that it's always best to give measurements!

However, everything worked out for the best because we decided that it would be an ideal item for a child's bedroom, both decorative and practical. We combined various nautical serviettes for this project, the idea behind it being to create a beach scene. We also tried a few experiments with fabric painting – they were successful but ended up giving us a lot more work. We suggest you read our handy hints before beginning and hopefully you will learn from our mistakes.

You will need

Cotton wall hanging
Selection of nautical serviettes
 – cut & separated
Plastic sheeting
Blue transparent fabric paint
Yellow transparent fabric paint
White fabric paint
Foam applicator
Small paintbrush
Flat, soft synthetic brush
Textile medium
Fabric sealer

1 Wash the wall hanging to get rid of any sizing and then iron it when dry. Place plastic inside the pockets of the wall hanging and paint each pocket using a sponge applicator and the blue and yellow paint. You may need to use the small brush to get into difficult corners. Leave to dry. Cover with a thin cloth and iron (dry cotton setting) to heat-seal.

2 Lay the beach and sea image in position and make markings where the beach meets the sea. Paint over the area that will become the beach with white paint. It won't cover completely but will lighten the area so that the blue doesn't show through too much.

3 Make up a fabric paint wash as follows: 1 part white fabric paint to 2 parts water. Use a brush to apply the wash over the painted areas, working from one side to the other. Leave to dry. The wash is very subtle and may have to be applied a few times before you get the desired effect. Leave to dry and heat-seal.

4 Lay the serviette motifs in position and begin gluing them down. Make a mark around the image (a few dabs of medium will do the trick) remove it and apply medium to the area where it will go. Place the motif on the wet area and begin gluing it down by brushing extra medium over it, using the synthetic brush. Work from one side of the image to the other. Continue applying all the motifs in this way. Leave to dry. Apply a coat of fabric sealer to the entire decorated area (for added protection) ,leave to dry and heat-seal as above.

HANDY HINTS

- The 'washed denim' look on the sky is easy to achieve but tends to run - thereby discolouring the area around it – which is why it's best to do it before you sew the wall hanging together. We really wish we'd known this before we did it. In order to achieve this look: rub over the wet paint with a damp cloth, taking out colour as you do so. A washed look can also be achieved by wetting the fabric before you begin painting.

- If your paint goes over onto the pocket surrounds (like it did with our washed look) you can cover it up with opaque paint. You may have to apply 2 coats to cover it (like we did!)

- We applied the white wash over the blue and yellow

paint to 'knock it back' a bit. You can use opaque paint for this because it is weakened by the water and therefore doesn't seem to interfere with the adhesion of the serviettes. On the other hand, if you like the colours as they are you don't have to apply a wash at all.

- Some of the serviette motifs were applied in reverse (wrong side down) to create mirror images.

- In some instances, where the serviette just wasn't long enough to go across the pockets, we added sections to complete the picture.

- When making something for children forget the 'less-is-more' concept. It doesn't apply to children. Replace it with 'the-busier-the-better'!

Rooster notice board

It was only once we'd started decorating the notice board that we noticed it was taking on a distinctly Mexican look, which just goes to prove that a lot of our projects and techniques happen by accident. It was fun to make until we started putting on the triangular border. Each piece was applied separately and, while this wasn't difficult, it was time-consuming and played havoc with our backs. We're pretty sure that standing and bending over it (instead of sitting) for about 4 hours had something to do with an appointment with the chiropractor the next day. We suggest that you take it in stages and get yourself a chair! Oh yes, and try not to get the green board paint all over your hands – it takes about 3 days to remove.

1 Prepare the notice board by following the instructions for preparation of new wood on page 23. Stir the green board paint thoroughly before using it – this could take a while but needs to be done. Use the paintbrush to apply the paint to the middle section of the notice board. Leave overnight to dry and then put on a second coat. If you have accidentally brushed green paint on the frame, rub it down with turpentine. Allow to dry.

2 Apply 2-3 coats of green-beige paint to the frame and back of the notice board, allowing drying time between coats. If you get paint on the already painted (green) area clean immediately with a damp cloth.

Seal the frame and back of the board with a coat of Podge and leave to dry.

3 Begin to apply the serviette images by placing them on the frame and brushing polyurethane varnish over them. Use the synthetic brush and work from one side of the image to the other. Be sure to line up the triangles on the sides otherwise things could end up looking untidy. When gluing down the little dots at the bottom, it's best to apply a dab of varnish to the frame and use a pair of tweezers to place and push the dot into position. When dry, seal the back and frame of the notice board with 2 coats of polyurethane varnish, allowing drying time between coats.

YOU WILL NEED

Wooden notice board
2 (Mexican) rooster serviettes
 – cut & separated
Green board paint
Paintbrush
Turpentine
Green-beige acrylic craft paint
Foam applicator
Podge
Flat, soft synthetic brush
Water-based polyurethane varnish

HANDY HINTS

- Whatever you do, don't put Podge or varnish over the green board paint in the middle otherwise you won't be able to write on it.
- In order to ensure good adhesion of images it's always a good idea to dab over them with a dry applicator while they're still wet.
- Always smooth out excess varnish around serviette images, otherwise you'll have ridges around them.
- When applying the triangles, stop before you get close to the end. They are not even sizes so you will to have to play around with the various pieces to make them fit. Cut some of them down if necessary.

Orange enamel bowl

We know we've already done a bowl for this book but they are so popular that we decided to slip in another one. The problem with decorating bowls is that once they are finished, they don't seem to hang around for very long. After all these years, neither one of us has a decoupaged bowl in our homes. Our friends, however, have plenty so let this be a lesson to you. Don't give your stuff away thinking that you'll make another, even better one for yourself when you've got the time – it just doesn't happen.

The beauty of working with serviette images on bowls is that even large ones mould so well to curved surfaces, unlike paper cut-outs which need a little persuasion to lie flat.

You WILL NEED
Enamel bowl
Orange serviettes –
   cut & separated
2 paintbrushes
Foam applicator
Broken white PVA paint
Raw umber artist's acrylic paint
Acrylic scumble glaze
Podge
Flat, soft synthetic brush
Water-based polyurethane hard
   varnish

1 Prepare the bowl according to the instructions for preparation of enamel on page 26. Apply 4 coats of broken white PVA, allowing drying time between coats. You can use a foam applicator for this.

2 Make up an antiquing mix of 1 part artist's acrylic, 2 parts scumble glaze and 3 parts water. Begin working on the inside of the bowl first and apply the mixture with a brush. Leave for about 1 minute and, before it dries, begin smoothing it out using the second dry brush. Leave it to dry completely and then repeat the process on the outside of the bowl. Apply a coat of Podge to the entire bowl in order to protect the paint. Leave to dry.

3 Apply the serviette images with the synthetic brush and varnish. Place the dry image in position and glue it down by brushing varnish over it. It's best to apply one strip of varnish down the middle of the image in order to centre it and then work from there outwards. Apply all the images in the same way and leave to dry.

4 Complete your project by applying 4-6 coats of varnish to the entire bowl, allowing sufficient drying time between coats.

HANDY HINTS

- If any of the leaves or stems break off when you're applying the images, simply add them on afterwards. You may have to cut new pieces if they're too damaged.
- You don't have to use the entire image – the orange images on the outside of the bowl were 'cut-down' in order to prevent the bowl from looking too busy.
- Be careful not to lean on any of the still wet images when working on the bowl as they will lift.
- We normally advise applying serviettes by working from one side to the other but when an image needs to be centred it's best to work from the middle outwards.

Boat storage bags

You will need

Storage bags (synthetic!)
Boat serviette – cut & separated
Calico fabric
Scissors
Iron-on magic appliqué
Baking paper
Textile medium
Flat, soft synthetic brush

We bought these storage bags from a well-known homeware store. It was only when we got home and undid the packaging that we realised that the fabric was purely synthetic. Now, after all this time, we know a thing or two about serviettes and one of them is that they don't adhere for any length of time to synthetics. However, this gave us an opportunity to come up with a way of overcoming the problem and we did, so don't discount working on synthetics – it can be done. The trick is to apply the image onto cotton fabric first and then sew it onto the item that you wish to decorate. Sneaky, eh? The laundry bag was easy because we made it ourselves so we knew it was cotton. The serviette we used had two different images on it so only one variety of serviette was needed for these three items.

Storage bags

1 Wash and iron the piece of fabric. Cut out a piece of appliqué the same size as the serviette image but don't peel off the backing paper. Place the appliqué onto an ironing board (coarse side facing up) and put the serviette over it with the printed side up. Cover with a piece of baking paper to protect your iron and the image and then iron the serviette onto the applique. Use a dry cotton setting.

2 Trim the edges of the serviette image, peel off the backing paper and position it onto the fabric. Cover it with baking paper and iron over it for about a minute to glue it to the fabric. Use the synthetic brush to cover the entire image with medium and ensure that you extend the medium over the edges. Leave to dry.

3 Cut the fabric so that you are left with a serviette image backed by fabric. Place it in position on the storage bag, tack it down to hold it in place and sew around the edges to secure it.

Laundry bag

1 Wash and iron the bag to remove sizing. Find the bottom centre of the bag (where the image will be placed) using a ruler and mark it with the fabric marker. Place the serviette image in position, make markings around it and remove it. Apply medium to the area where the image will be placed, extending it up to the markings. Place the serviette back into position and glue it down by brushing more medium over it. Use the synthetic brush to apply one strip of medium down the centre, working over to one side and then the other. Leave to dry.

2 Use a ruler and fabric marker to mark the areas where the stripes will be. Apply masking tape around the image and in strips down the bag, pressing it down firmly so that paint can't seep underneath. Place plastic sheeting inside the bag to

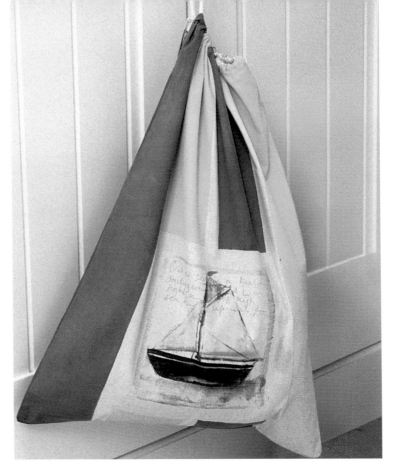

prevent paint from seeping through and behind the bag as well to protect your work surface. Paint the masked areas, ensuring that you keep a wet edge while you are working to avoid streaking. Leave to dry.

3 Turn the bag over and repeat the process on the back, ensuring that you match up the lines when you mask off. Leave to dry. Remove all the masking tape and iron on the reverse side to heat-seal (dry cotton setting).

YOU WILL NEED
Calico laundry bag
Boat serviette – cut & separated
Ruler
Water-soluble fabric marker
Textile medium
Flat, soft synthetic brush
Masking tape
Plastic sheet
Blue fabric paint
Sandy yellow fabric paint
Foam applicator

Rose scatter cushions

"One of the quickest ways to transform the character of a room is by changing or adding scatter cushions in complementary or contrasting colours." Virtually every house makeover book ever published has this helpful advice somewhere inside its pages. This is all very well in theory until you see the cost of one cushion, let alone the five or six you'll need to make any visible difference whatsoever.

Decorating your own will save you a lot of money and you won't feel guilty about changing them six months later if you get tired of them. These cushions were made out of bleached calico with batting inserted into the edges to add interest. In almost all cases we made the items (or had them made by our seamstress – we gave her the correct measurements this time!) before we began painting and decorating. However, it would often make a lot more sense to decorate the pieces first, before sewing them together. Always wash your fabric before beginning to sew as this sorts out any problems with shrinkage and removes the sizing.

If you have any plain cotton scatter cushions lying around at home you can use this method to give them a face-lift.

1 Insert plastic inside the cushion so that paint doesn't bleed through to the other side. Paint both sides of the cushion (use the applicator) with ivory paint, allowing the first side to dry before painting the other. Leave to dry. As the cushion can't be heat-sealed properly by turning it inside out, cover it with a thin cloth or baking paper and iron over it (dry cotton setting) to heat-seal the paint.

2 Place the motif in the centre of the cushion, mark around it with the fabric marker and remove it. Use the synthetic brush to apply a coat of medium to the marked area. Apply the motif by placing one side of it into position on the moistened area and brush over it with extra medium. Work towards the middle then over to the other side, extending the medium slightly beyond the edges of the motif. Leave to dry.

3 Cover the image with cloth or baking paper and iron over it (dry cotton setting again) to heat-seal and bob's your uncle!

YOU WILL NEED

Calico scatter cushion
Rose serviette – cut & separated
Plastic sheet
Ivory fabric paint (transparent)
Foam applicator
Water-soluble fabric marker
Textile medium
Flat, soft synthetic brush

HANDY HINTS

- You can smooth out most of the wrinkles with your fingers but make sure that the image is wet with medium otherwise you'll damage it.
- If any of the edges lift over time, simply reapply medium and heat-seal.
- If the cushion is going to take a battering (like in a child's room) apply a coat of fabric paint sealer for added protection.
- The cushion should be hand-washed only, in lukewarm water.

Pumpkin shopping bags

By making and decorating your own shopping bags, instead of buying those plastic ones, you can do your own little bit for the environment. These were made of hessian and lined with calico to give them added strength and durability. Lots of fellow shoppers have asked us where they can buy these bags because they're unique and hold a lot of shopping. So, for those of you who are looking for a sideline to make some extra money, here's a perfect opportunity. Just remember to post us a cheque for 25% of the profits! The same serviette, applied in different ways gives you an idea of how versatile serviette decoupage is.

Bag with cut out images

1 Place plastic inside the bags before you begin applying the serviettes. This prevents the medium from seeping through to the other side of the bag. Cut out the serviette images and separate the layers as only the top one is used. Arrange them on the bag. Then, working on one image at a time, mark its position by dabbing medium around it. Remove the image and apply medium to the area where it will be placed. Replace the image and glue it down by brushing medium over it. Ensure that you extend the medium slightly beyond the edges to ensure good adhesion. Apply the rest of the images in this way and leave to dry.

Bag with single image

1 Cut a square from the serviette and separate the layers so that you are only left with the top one. Apply a coat of medium to the area where the image is to be placed. Lay the serviette down on the moistened area and begin gluing it down by brushing medium over it. Centre the image by applying a strip of medium down the centre, working over to one side first and then the other. Leave to dry.

2 Heat-seal both bags by covering them with a thin cloth and ironing over them. The iron should be on a dry cotton setting.

YOU WILL NEED
Hessian bag
2 pumpkin serviettes
Scissors
Plastic sheet
Textile medium
Flat, soft synthetic brush

> ### HANDY HINTS
> - A running stitch was used to add interest to one of the bags. It's best to make markings on the bag with a water-soluble marker to ensure that your stitches are evenly spaced. The marks can be removed with water.
> - Hessian is extremely porous (and takes a long time to dry) so be prepared to use more medium than you usually would.